The Handbook
of
Vermont Shrubs
and Woody Vines

By L. R. Jones and F. V. Rand
Illustrated by Mary Robinson

with an Introduction to the
new edition by
Raymond T. Foulds, Jr.
Extension Forester, University of Vermont

CHARLES E. TUTTLE COMPANY
Rutland, Vermont and Tokyo, Japan

REPRESENTATIVES:

For Continental Europe:
BOXERBOOKS, INC., Zurich

For the British Isles:
PRENTICE-HALL INTERNATIONAL, INC., London

For Australasia:
BOOK WISE (AUSTRALIA) PTY. LTD.
104-108 Sussex Street, Sydney 2000

Published by the Charles E. Tuttle Company, Inc.
of Rutland, Vermont and Tokyo, Japan
with editorial offices at
Suido 1-chome, 2-6, Bunkyo-ku, Tokyo

Library of Congress Catalog Card No. 79-84806

International Standard Book No. 0-8048-1316-7

First edition published in 1909
by the Vermont Agricultural Experiment Station,
College of Agriculture, University of Vermont.

First Tuttle edition 1979

Printed in USA

Cover design by Margaret E. McIntyre

BULLETIN 145: VERMONT SHRUBS AND WOODY VINES

By L. R. Jones and F. V. Rand[1]

ILLUSTRATED BY MARY ROBINSON

Table of Contents

Key for determining Vermont Shrubs and Woody
Vines 6-10
Pine Family 11-14
    Common juniper 12
    Shrubby red juniper 13
    American yew 13
Sweet-gale Family 14-15
    Sweet-fern 14
    Sweet-gale 15
Willow Family.. 16-22
    Pussy willow 20
    Beaked willow 20
    Prairie willow 20
    Shining willow 21
    Heart-leaved willow 21
    Purple osier willow 22
    The less common willows 22
Oak Family 23-27
    Hoary alder 24
    Smooth alder 25
    Green alders 25
    Beaked hazelnut 26
    American hazelnut 27

[1] The account of the Rose family was largely prepared by Mr. W. W. Eggleston, who also read the entire manuscript and made helpful suggestions at numerous points. Use has also been made of the data accumulated by Mr. Harmon Sheldon, of the class of 1907 of the University of Vermont, whose senior thesis was upon Vermont Shrubs. The authors make grateful acknowledgement of their indebtedness to these gentlemen.

i

Crowfoot Family 28-29
    Virgin's bower 28
    Purple clematis 28
Barberry Family 30
    Common barberry 30
Moonseed Family 31
    Moonseed 31
Laurel Family 32-33
    Spice-bush 32
Saxifrage Family 33-38
    Smooth gooseberry 35
    Prickly gooseberry 36
    Swamp gooseberry 37
    Red currant 37
    Black currant 37
    Mountain currant 38
Witch-hazel Family 38-40
    Witch-hazel 38
Rose Family 40-70
    Sand cherry 42
    Appalachian cherry 43
    Steeple bush 44
    Meadow sweet 45
    Chokeberry 46
    Black chokeberry 46
    Serviceberry 46
    Rock shad-bush 47
    Shore shad-bush 47
    Mountain shad-bush 49
    Shrubby cinquefoil 49
    Three-toothed cinquefoil 50
    Flowering raspberry 52
    Red raspberry 52
    Black raspberry 55
    High-bush blackberry 58

Recurved blackberry 58
Mountain blackberry 58
Red dewberry 59
Bristly dewberry 59
Black dewberry 60
Swamp dewberry 60
Cultivated berries 60
Cinnamon rose 62
Sweetbrier rose 63
Swamp rose 64
Pasture rose 64
Smooth rose 65
Cultivated roses 66
Thornapples 66
Rue Family .... 70 -72
Prickly ash 71
Crowberry Family 72
Black crowberry 72
Sumach Family .... 72 -78
Staghorn sumach 73
Smooth sumach 74
Dwarf sumach 74
Fragrant sumach 76
Poison ivy 76
Poison sumach 78
Holly Family .... 78 -80
Winterberry 79
Mountain holly 79
Staff-tree Family .... 80 -82
Climbing bittersweet 80
Maple Family 82
Bladder-nut 82
Buckthorn Family .... 83 -84
Alder-leaved buckthorn 83
New Jersey tea 84
Smaller red-root 84
Vine Family .... 85 -89
River grape 85

Summer grape 87
Fox grape 87
Virginia creepers 88
Tendril creeper 89
Disk creeper 89
Rock-rose Family 89-90
Beach heather 89
Mezereum Family 90-91
Leatherwood 90
Daphne 91
Oleaster Family 91
Canadian buffalo-berry 91
Loosestrife Family 91-92
Swamp loosestrife 91
Dogwood Family 92-99
Flowering dogwood 93
Bunchberry 94
Alternate-leaved dogwood 95
Round-leaved dogwood 96
Silky dogwood 97
Red-ozier dogwood 97
Panicled dogwood 99
Heath Family 99-121
Bearberry 101
Wintergreen 101
Creeping snowberry 103
Huckleberry 103
Common highbush blueberry 105
Black blueberry 106
Canada blueberry 106
Early low blueberry 107
Late low blueberry 109
Mountain blueberries 110
Large cranberry 111
Small cranberry 112
Mountain cranberry 112
Wild rosemary 113

Male berry 113
Leather leaf 114
Trailing arbutus 114
Mountain laurel 117
Pale laurel 118
Sheep laurel 118
Labrador tea 118
Great rhododendron 119
Pink azalea 120
Rhodora 121
Olive Family 121
    Introduced shrubs (privets, fringe-tree, forsythia, lilacs). 121
Nightshade Family 122-123
    Climbing nightshade 122
Madder Family 123-125
    Button-bush 124
Honeysuckle Family 125-135
    Twin-flower 125
    Bush-honeysuckle 125
    Snowberry 126
    Glaucous honeysuckle 128
    Hairy honeysuckle 129
    Blue honeysuckle 129
    Swamp honeysuckle 129
    Fly honeysuckle 129
    Tartarian honeysuckle 130
    Common elder 132
    Red-berried elder 134
Arrow-wood Family 135-142
    High cranberry-bush 137
    Few-flowered cranberry-bush 137
    Hobble-bush 138
    Maple-leaved arrow-wood 139
    Downy arrow-wood 140
    Toothed arrow-wood 140
    Withe-rod 140
    Sheep-berry 141

The Handbook
of
Vermont Shrubs
and Woody Vines

INTRODUCTION

This was formerly Bulletin No. 145 of the Vermont Agricultural Experiment Station, published in October, 1909. The senior author, Lewis Ralph Jones, was Botanist at the Station, with headquarters at the Williams Science Hall, University of Vermont. He was an author of many publications on trees and shrubs, and did much research on plant diseases, especially those of the potato plant.

He lived in Vermont for 20 years (1889-1910). Later he was at the University of Wisconsin for over 25 years. He retired to Brookfield, Vt. in about 1936. The L. R. Jones State Forest in Marshfield, Vt. is named after him.

The junior author was F. V. Rand, who prepared the key in the front of the book and an explanation of how to use the key. He did the work while a Junior and Senior at the University.

Illustrations (line drawings) are by Miss Mary Robinson, who was also a Junior and Senior at the University of Vermont while doing the work.

Dr. Ezra Brainerd advised in the treatment of the blackberry group and read proofs.

Mr. W. W. Eggleston made suggestions throughout and wrote much of the Chapter on the Rose family.

This bulletin was issued 10 years after the bulletin Trees of Vermont (No. 73). One was meant to supplement the other.

In the front of the Handbook there is a Table of Contents which lists thirty Families of the plants which are described.

The Handbook includes introduced species of special interest as well as native species. There are 147 pages. There is an alphabetical index at the end.

Some of the data on shrubs is from a senior thesis by Hermon Sheldon of the UVM Class of 1907.

The Handbook contains material for readers who have little or no botanical training, but who wish to learn the names of the plants and the main facts about their occurrence and characters. Edible characters, poisonous nature, and ornamental values are mentioned. Detailed also is how Indians and early settlers alike used plant life as sources of healing medicines —and— materials for craft and woodworking skills.

In the arrangement of families and the choice of botanical names the usage of Gray's Manual of Botany is followed. The usage of the Britton manual is followed for many of the English names. Local custom is also followed in some cases.

The Handbook has several features useful to the reader that are not often found in other similar bulletins. These include the key and its explanation; the line drawings of leaves, fruit and some flowers; and explanation of uses in woodcraft and handicraft.

RAYMOND T. FOULDS, JR.
Extension Forester
University of Vermont

INTRODUCTION

It is now just ten years since this station issued bulletin 73, The Trees of Vermont. Three years later bulletin 94 appeared on Vermont Grasses and Clovers. The present publication is the third in the series having a like general aim. It includes an account of the native shrubs and woody vines, with briefer mention of such introduced species as are of especial interest. Like the earlier publications it is primarily addressed to readers who have little or no botanical training, but who wish to learn the names of these plants as well as the main facts relative to their occurrence and characters. In this connection especial attention has been given to any matters of human relation such as edible qualities, poisonous nature, ornamental values, etc. In numerous cases pains has been taken to record facts concerning the use of these plants made by the Indians or the early settlers, for such purposes as dyeing and basketry. These things are of sufficient historical and educational worth to justify the space thus given to them; but, in addition, it seems probable that the revival of interest in the handicrafts, which is coming with industrial education, is prophetic of a return to the usage of some of these things. Certainly it is a wholesome thing for all of us to be reminded of such matters of early woodcraft.

This bulletin does not bear so directly as have the earlier ones of the series upon problems of practical agriculture and forestry, although it is clearly pertinent to such problems. It is the needs of the boys and girls of Vermont farms and villages and of their teachers in the rural schools that have been uppermost in mind in the preparation of these pages. Every such school ground has a natural setting of shrubs and vines; every roadside leading to it is fringed with natural growths that rival in aesthetic charm the finest plantations of the city parks. It is pitiful to realize that for the children educated in this environment the names and values of these things are a sealed book. What are we to say of progress in our educational methods when the school boy, yes and his teacher too, have not only less knowledge about these matters, but what is more lamentable less intelligent interest in them, than did his grandparents or even the Indian boy who once played in these same valleys. Quite apart from any mere practical applications of the information to human problems it is worth while to make any contribution possible to a change of attitude toward nature study, and one of the most important advance steps toward this goal will be made when each questioner realizes that there is within his reach the means of securing reliable answers to his inquiries. With this in view keys have been prepared with so little reference to the more obscure or minute botanical characters that it is hoped careful observers may identify an unknown plant.

The method of using the "keys" will probably be evident to most; yet lest any reader should be puzzled, an explanation of their use is given at the bottom of the next page. The matter of discriminating between related species has been simplified and the pages made clearer as well as more attractive by illustrations.

In the arrangement of families and the choice of botanical names, the usage of the Gray New Manual of Botany is followed. Where the names of earlier standard works or of other modern texts, including the Britton Manual, differ from this, the synonymy is entered in parentheses. For many of the English names the usage of the Britton Manual has been followed, and where local custom departs from that of the botanical texts the aim has been to recognize it.

Our associates in the preparation of this bulletin, Mr. Rand and Miss Robinson, worked upon the details during their Junior and Senior years as the students at this University. It is but justice not only to acknowledge their conscientious collaboration but also to record the fact that this was largely a labor of love inspired primarily by their interest in the work, the satisfactory completion of which is their chief recompense. The writer wishes here to record his own appreciation of their assistance as well as that of Dr. Ezra Brainerd, who has advised in the treatment of the blackberry group and read proofs, and of Mr. W. W. Eggleston, who has made suggestions throughout and written much of the chapter on the difficult rose family.

L. R. Jones.

6 THE HANDBOOK OF

KEY FOR DETERMINING VERMONT SHRUBS AND WOODY VINES[1]

PREPARED BY F. V. RAND

1. Vines, i. e. stems climbing, creeping or trailing; not self-supporting 2
1. Shrubs, i. e. stems erect or reclining 11

2. Climbing over some support 3
2. Stems trailing or creeping on the ground 7

3. Climbing by twining stems 4
3. Climbing by tendrils situated opposite the leaves.......... 6
3. Climbing by roots produced wherever the stem touches a proper support ....Poison Ivy, p. 76
3. Climbing by leaf-stalks clasping support....Virgin's Bower, p. 28
3. Climbing by simply growing over the support.
Climbing Nightshade, Solanum, p. 95

4. Leaves opposite, i. e. 2 at each joint or node of the stem.
Glaucous Honeysuckle, p. 128
4. Leaves alternate, i. e. one at each joint or node 5

5. Leaves pinnately veined, margins toothed.
Bittersweet, Celastrus, p. 80
5. Leaves palmately veined, lobed, with margins otherwise entire ....Moonseed Vine, 83

6. Leaves simple ....Grape, p. 85
6. Leaves compound ....Virginia Creeper, p. 88

---

[1] Since the method of using a "key" like the above may not be clear to all, a word of explanation is added. Its purpose is to aid in determining the name of any strange Vermont shrub or woody vine. Suppose the unknown plant before you is a woody vine as characterized in the first line under "1" at the head of the "key"; you should then pass down to "2." Next note its habit; if its stems tend to climb over the support rather than to trail or creep on the ground you should pass on to "3" below. Here you must decide between the five types described. Suppose it climbs by roots produced wherever the stem touches a proper support such as the bark of a tree, you have the Poison Ivy and should turn to p. 128, for fuller description. If, however, it climbs by the leaf-stalks clasping the support, it is the Virgin's Bower and is described on p. 80. If, on the other hand it has tendrils, you must pass on to "6," where, according to character of leaf, you learn that your vine is either a Wild Grape or a Virginia Creeper.

7. Leaves simple, evergreen 8
7. Leaves compound ....Dewberry, p. 59

8. Leaves saw-toothed, teeth bristle-tipped, aromatic.
                                   Wintergreen, p. 101
8. Leaves not as above 9

9. Leaves with margin distinctly revolute, i. e. rolled backward. 10
9. Leaves with margin not revolute......Arbutus, Mayflower, p. 114

10. Fruit aromatic, white ....Creeping Snowberry, p. 103
10. Fruit not as above 11

11. Leaves linear-oblong; fruit black.......Black Crowberry, p. 72
11. Leaves oval, ovate, or obovate; fruit reddish....Cranberry, p. 111

12. Reclining shrubs 13
12. Erect shrubs 15

13. Leaves deciduous ....Mountain Currant, p. 38
13. Leaves evergreen 14

14. Leaves scale-like or awl-shaped ....Juniper, p. 12
14. Leaves not as above ....Bearberry, p. 101

15. Leaves evergreen or persistent 16
15. Leaves deciduous 23

16. Leaves 1-12 inch long ....Hudsonia, Beach Heather, p. 89
16. Leaves much more than 1-12 inch long 17

17. Leaves not over 1-12 inch broad 18
17. Leaves much over 1-12 inch broad 12

18. Leaves awl-shaped, needle-pointed; mature fruit a bluish
     berry ....Juniper, p. 11
18. Leaves flattened, not sharp, borne in a hemlock-like spray;
     mature fruit a red berry........Ground Hemlock, Yew, p. 13

19. Leaves densely brown-woolly below........Labrador Tea, p. 118
19. Leaves not as above 20

20. Flowers in a long one-sided spray...........Leatherleaf, p. 114
20. Flowers not as above 21

21. Fruit-pod (capsule) distinctly oblong; flowers large and
     showy, 1½ to 2 inches across.......Great Rhododendron, p. 119
21. Fruit-pod (capsule) globular or nearly so; flowers smaller.... 22

22. Buds naked; flowers showy, purple or pink; corolla ½ to 1
    inch across ....Smaller Laurels, Kalmia, p. 117
22. Buds scaly; flowers rather inconspicuous, white; corolla not
    over ¼ inch across........Wild Rosemary, Andromeda, p. 113

23. Leaves simple 31
23. Leaves compound 24

24. Leaves opposite 25
24. Leaves alternate 26

25. Fruit (capsule) having 3 large inflated cells...Bladder-nut, p. 82
25. Fruit a berry ....Common Elder, p. 132

26. Leaves without stipules; flowers small, greenish..Sumach, p. 72
26. Leaves with stipules 27

27. Small, greenish flowers in early spring before the leaves;
    leaves and bark pungent-aromatic ....Prickly Ash, p. 71
27. Flowers, yellow or pink in early summer; plants not
    aromatic 28

28. Fruit edible ....Blackberry and Raspberry, p. 52
28. Fruits not edible 29

29. Flowers large, pink ....Rose, p. 62
29. Flowers small, yellow or white 30

30. Flowers in pyramidal clusters...........Siberian Spiraea, p. 43
30. Flowers not as above ....Cinquefoil, Potentilla, p. 49

31. Leaves opposite or whorled, i. e. two or more at each joint or
    node of the stem 32
31. Leaves alternate, i. e. only one at each joint or node 39

32. Fruit dry 33
32. Fruit pulpy 35

33. Flower and fruit in a dense, perfectly spherical head.
                                          Button-bush, p. 124
33. Flower and fruit not as above 34

34. Flowers in a long pyramidal cluster...............Lilac, p. 121
34. Flowers not as above........Bush Honeysuckle, Diervilla, p. 125

35. Young shoots and under side of leaves brown-scurfy.
                                          Buffalo-berry, p. 91
35. Leaves and shoots not as above 36

36. Fruit with a single stone 37
36. Fruit with two or more seeds 38

37. Fruit with a more or less flattened stone; flowers 5-parted.
Viburnum, p. 135
37. Fruit with a globular or ovoid, two-seeded stone; flowers 4-
parted ....Dogwood, p. 92
38. Berry snow-white with two seeds.............Snowberry, p. 126
38. Berry reddish or bluish-black with several seeds.
Honeysuckle, Lonicera, p. 125
39. Leaves palmately-veined 40
39. Leaves pinnately-veined 41
40. Flowers large, pink; fruit thimble-shaped.
Flowering Raspberry, p. 52
40. Flowers small, yellow, green or purple; fruit globose.
Currant, Gooseberry, p. 35-37
41. Leaves lobed, fragrant ....Sweet Fern, p. 14
41. Leaves entire or toothed 42
42. Leaves sharply spiny-toothed ....Barberry, p. 30
42. Leaves not spiny-toothed 43
43. Branches armed with sharp thorns..........Thorn-apple, p. 66
43. Branches not as above 44
44. Leaves and bark strongly aromatic when crushed.
Spice-bush, p. 32
44. Leaves and bark not aromatic 45
45. Bark exceedingly thick, leathery and tough; buds hidden under the base of the leaf stalks ....Leatherwood, p. 90
45. Bark and buds not as above 46
46. Twigs and leaves clammy with resinous dots when young.
Huckleberry, p. 103
46. Twigs and leaves not as above 47
47. Buds inclosed in a single scale; flowers and fruit borne in
catkins ....Willow, p. 16
47. Buds and flowers not as above 48
48. Leaves distinctly one-sided or oblique, at the base, wavy-
margined; yellow flowers in late autumn, fruit ripening the
following season ....Witch Hazel, p. 38
48. Leaves not distinctly one-sided at the base; flowers not yellow; fruit maturing the same season 49
49. Flowers in catkins 50
49. Flowers not as above 52

50. Fruit an edible nut ....Hazelnut, p. 26
50. Fruit not as above 51

51. Fruit a small cone ....Alder, p. 24
51. Fruit not a cone ....Sweet Gale, p. 15

52. Fruit dry 60
52. Fruit fleshy 53

53. Fruit with a single stone 54
53. Fruit not as above 56

54. Stone two-seeded..............Alternate-leaved Dogwood, p. 95
54. Stone one-seeded 55

55. Drupe red; flowers before leaves....Lady Laurel, Daphne, p. 91
55. Drupe brownish or black; flowers with leaves......Cherry, p. 42

56. Fruit red or purple when mature 57
56. Fruit blue or black when mature 59

57. Fruit 10-seeded, edible ....Shadbush, p. 47
57. Fruit 5 to 6 seeded, not edible 58

58. Berries borne on a long stalk.............Mountain Holly, p. 79
58. Berries without stalk (sessile) ....Winterberry, p. 79

59. Flowers bell-shaped; fruit sweet and edible......Blueberry, p. 105
59. Flowers and fruit not as above.......................... 60

60. Flowers white; fruit slightly astringent.......Chokeberry, p. 46
60. Flowers yellow-green; fruit very astringent, inedible.
                              Buckthorn, p. 83

61. Flowers small 62
61. Flowers large, 1 to 2 inches across.
                    Swamp Pink, Azalea, Rhodora, p. 120

62. Flowers urn-shaped ....Male Berry, p. 113
62. Flowers saucer-shaped 63

63. Flowers and fruit in narrow pyramidal clusters, 4 to 8 inches
       long ....Hardhack, Spiraea, p. 44
63. Flowers and fruit in rounded or flat clusters, 1 to 2 inches
       long ....New Jersey Tea, Redroot, p. 84

PINE FAMILY. CONIFERAE [1]

The plants of the pine family are nearly all evergreen trees, the pines, spruces, hemlocks, etc. They are characterized by their cone-like fruit and needle or scale-shaped leaves. Most of them are therefore described in an earlier bulletin, "Trees of Vermont."[2]

Three of these, however, are evergreen shrubs as they occur in Vermont, namely, the two junipers and the yew. The junipers and yew differ from the other Vermont conifers in having fleshy, berry-like fruits instead of dry, scaly cones. The young juniper berries are grayish-white, becoming bluish as they ripen, while those of the yew are green when young and turn to a beautifully bright coral-red in late summer.

THE JUNIPERS

There are three species of juniper in Vermont, the "red cedar," a well known and valuable tree, which has an upright trunk typically 20 to 40 feet high (see "Trees of Vermont") and the following two shrubs.

KEY FOR DISTINGUISHING THE TWO SHRUBBY JUNIPERS

Scale-like leaves spreading in whorls of three, berry-like fruits borne on the sides of the twigs (lateral)............Common juniper.
Scale-like leaves pressed close to stem, mostly opposite, berry-like fruits on the end of twig (terminal)........Shrubby red cedar.

---

[1] The so-called "ground pines" are low evergreen plants common in Vermont woods and so closely resembling small pines and spruces that to avoid confusion they deserve mention here. There are several kinds but all are quite similar in general character. The branches, thickly covered with evergreen scale-like leaves, rise a few inches above the ground, either in small clusters or borne on an extensively creeping cord-like stem. The fruits on the commonest species are borne on slender cone-like clusters, one-eighth inch in diameter by one inch long, terminating the upper branches. The commoner species with trailing stems are frequently gathered in late autumn for making holiday wreaths, and hence are termed "Christmas greens." Although having so close a resemblance to the conifers they really belong to the fern family and are best called club moss or Lycopodium.

[2] "The Trees of Vermont," Vt. Sta. Bul. 73 (1899). This contains descriptions of all Vermont trees and, since it supplements the present bulletin at many points, it will frequently be referred to in this text. It may be secured and without charge so long as the now somewhat limited supply lasts. Address Experiment Station, Burlington, Vt.

COMMON JUNIPER. *Juniperus communis* L. var. *depressa* Pursh.

The common spreading juniper is frequent on dry hillsides and in rocky or sandy pastures of the Connecticut and Champlain valleys.   Indeed it is often so abundant as to be a nuisance. It is a low outspread evergreen shrub, seldom over two or three feet high but often broadening into circular beds five to ten feet across.   The horizontal branches lie half-buried in the soil and are frequently rooted so as to make the cluster difficult to eradicate.   The leaves are green below and whitish above, arranged in a whorl of three, standing out nearly at right angles to the branch.   They are one-third to one-half inch long, and have sharp rigid points which make contact with this shrub about as unpleasant as with a thistle.   This probably aids in protecting the plant from disturbance by grazing animals and so contributes to its aggres-

COMMON JUNIPER.
Fruiting branch, × ½.

siveness as a pasture weed.   Little use is made of the juniper in America.   In Europe, where people are more frugal, some value is attached to the wood, the bark affords material for rope-making and the berries are used for preparing gin and for medicinal drinks, esteemed in kidney troubles.   This juniper has some value for ornamental planting where a low cover is desired on a warm dry slope.   An upright form of it sometimes occurs in Massachusetts and may be expected especially in southern Vermont.   European columnar forms, particularly the Swedish juniper, are used ornamentally.

SHRUBBY RED JUNIPER. *Juniperus horizontalis* Moench. (*J. Sabina* var. *procumbens* Pursh.)

This is a semi-prostrate or creeping shrub, seldom more than four feet high, usually with long trailing branches bearing numerous short branchlets. It has a close resemblance, except in its prostrate habit, to the common red juniper or "red cedar" tree. (See "Trees of Vermont." p. 46.) It has been found in only two places in the State, West Rutland and Manchester, and since it has no economic interest, it will be given only this brief notice. It is a matter of botanical concern, however, to learn further as to its distribution and any one finding it should report it to the botanists at the ·University of Vermont or elsewhere for verification and record.

GROUND HEMLOCK. AMERICAN YEW. *Taxus canadensis* Marsh.

The lover of rich colors must always rejoice when he comes upon a bed of the ground hemlock with its deep green foliage and bright red fruit. It is frequent throughout Vermont on

AMERICAN YEW OR GROUND HEMLOCK.
Fruiting branch, × ½.

cool moist banks under the shade of other evergreens. It is a low straggling shrub, the stems often trailing six or eight feet with upright branches only half that length. The foliage is much like the hemlock tree, hence its name. Like this, the leaves are narrow and flat and appear to be two-ranked, giving a light spray-like effect. They are, however, somewhat larger and darker colored than those of the hemlock tree, so as quickly to attract the attention. In autumn the red pulpy berries about one-fourth of an inch in diameter stud the branches like coral beads and at once serve to distinguish this from any other Vermont plant. Practically no use is made of the yew in Vermont. It is, however, worthy of planting for ornamental purposes, especially on cool moist banks under partial shade where few other plants can rival its rich combination of evergreen foliage and red fruit. The berries are sometimes reputed as poisonous. There is some evidence that the leaves, if browsed, may injure animals and that the seed also contains a similar poison, but the pulp of the berries is edible.

SWEET-GALE FAMILY.   MYRICACEAE

Vermont has two shrubs of this family, each attractive in its way, but neither generally common. They are readily separable by the shape of their leaves. As shown in the accompanying sketches, the sweet-fern has a leaf three to six inches long, deeply cut into many rounded lobes, whereas the sweet-gale leaf is small and only slightly toothed. Closely allied to these is the bayberry or wax-myrtle of Massachusetts and southward, which produces berries so richly coated with wax that they have been used for making candles and soap.

SWEET-FERN. *Myrica asplenifolia* L.

This is a shrub about one to three feet high with slender finely cut leaves, as described above, that give it a fern-like appearance. When crushed, these have a strong spicy aroma, hence its common name was well chosen although actually it is not a fern. The fragrance of the dry leaf when burned is familiar to many New England boys. The flowering catkins are abundant in early spring but are less conspicuous than the green burr-like fruit in midsummer. It is so common as to deserve its rating as a weed in the dry sandy pastures and on sterile hills at the lower altitudes of the Champlain and Connecticut valleys. In the earlier days of home remedies, sweet-fern had its place in the preparation of diet-drinks and herb medicines because of its tonic and astringent properties, being used internally for colic and externally as a liniment for bruises and rheumatic ailments.

SWEET-GALE. *Myrica Gale* L.

The sweet-gale is a little taller than the sweet-fern with simple narrow leaves one to two inches long, dark green above

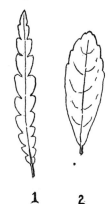

1   2
1. SWEET FERN.
2. SWEET GALE, × ⅔.

and pale below. It is frequent in Vermont in cool swamps and bordering ponds of the lower altitudes. It has no economic value in America although in the earlier days an infusion of the leaves or berries was sometimes used as a remedy for the itch and as a vermifuge. An infusion of the leaves is also sometimes used in Europe as an insecticide and it is said that the leaves if placed in drawers will keep out moths. The Canadian Indians used the young buds to dye their porcupine quills and all parts of the plant may be used in dyeing and tanning. In northern Europe the leaves are sometimes substituted for hops in brewing.

WILLOW FAMILY. SALICACEAE

This family includes the willows and poplars. The characters of each of these are so similar that any close observer soon distinguishes a willow or a poplar at sight. But it is quite another thing to know which willow or which poplar is before one. The species are all dioecious, that is the stamens and pistils are borne on different plants. As a result the poplars are dependent on wind and the willows on insects for pollination. Natural hybrids are more frequent than is commonly known, between the closely related species of willow. Hence any botanical student who will undertake their critical study will find interesting problems in nearly every swamp or wayside thicket. All of the poplars and four of the willows of Vermont have the habit and size of trees and are included in "Trees of Vermont" (pages 49-53). Of these the black willow is the only

one which will confuse the person who is trying to recognize the shrubby species. This black variety is the commonest willow tree overhanging the stream banks and growing along lake shores and the younger sprouts often form shrubby thickets. This cut from the tree bulletin is therefore included here to aid in distinguishing it. There are in addition some fifteen species of willows in Vermont which are more properly termed shrubs. It is no simple matter even for the skilled botanist to distinguish with certainty these fifteen

BLACK WILLOW.

Mature leaf and flowering twigs, × ⅓.
(From Trees of Vt., p. 50).

shrubby kinds. Fortunately for the beginner, only six of them are at all common. So if one groups the tree species by themselves and focuses his attention on the characters outlined on page 70 he may hope soon to recognize the common shrubby species.

PUSSY OR GLACOUS WILLOW.

Staminate or pollen bearing branch at right, pistillate or seed-bearing
at left, about natural size. Below at the left are single flowers of
the two kinds, twice natural size.

KEY TO THE SIX COMMON SHRUBBY WILLOWS

(Based primarily on characters of mature leaves)

1. Mature leaves woolly or soft-hairy on under side..............2
1. Mature leaves smooth on under side 3
2. Leaves rather broad in proportion to length (length 2-3 × width)
widest at about the middle, apex acute, margins flat or
wavy. A large shrub of wide range ....Beaked willow.
2. Leaves narrower in proportion to length (length 3-4 × width)
widest above middle, apex bluntish, margins rolled down.
a small shrub of dry sand plains ....Prairie willow.
3. Leaves whitish (glaucous) on under side......................4
3. Leaves green on under side 5
4. Leaves bluish-green above, long and narrow (length 6 × width
or more), finely toothed, introduced for basketry, not common ....Purple willow.
4. Leaves bright green above, broader in proportion to length
(length 3-4 × width) coarser toothed, a native shrub, common ....Pussy willow
5. Leaves shining as if polished, smooth even when young, stipules
small and inconspicuous ....Shining willow.
5. Leaves not shining, usually silky-hairy when young, stipules
relatively large ....Heart-leaved willow.

The willows are remarkable for the length, toughness and
vitality of their roots and for the readiness with which broken
branches strike root and throw up new shoots. For these reasons
they are nature's best covering to hold river banks, for which purpose the introduced tree species are preferable in most places.
The bark possesses a bitter tonic principle (salicine) which may
replace quinine in medicine and is also rich in tannin. The greatest
economic usage of the willows is, however, as a source of osiers
for making basketry and furniture. For landscape planting the
willows have value but the shrubs are not of so much worth as
the viburnums and dogwoods. The shining willow is the best
for foliage effect and the beaked willow has a place where large
mass effects are desired on drier ground. The European species
which have been improved by long selection are, however, generally preferable to the natives for ornamental and other uses.

LEAVES OF THE SIX COMMON SHRUBBY WILLOWS, × ½.

A, Heart-leaved willow;   D, Beaked willow;
B, Shining willow;   E, Prairie willow;
C, Purple osier willow;   F, Pussy or glaucous willow.

PUSSY OR GLAUCOUS WILLOW. *Salix discolor* Muhl.

This is the favorite pussy willow, conspicuous everywhere in early spring along streams and in moist wayside thickets. All of the willows have their flowers in similar catkins, but no other of the early ones is so large and bright as this. The staminate, or pollen-bearing catkins are bright yellow, while on other plants at the same time occur the duller ones which are pistillate and in May ripen the crop of downy seeds. This glaucous willow is one of the largest of the shrubby willows, often ten to twenty feet high, and the branches and foliage are relatively coarse. The leaves are often three to five inches long and are characterized, as explained in the key, by being bright green above and glaucous or whitish beneath, whence its name. The buds also are large and dark colored. Sometimes it is tree-like in habit.

BEAKED WILLOW. *Salix rostrata* Rich. (*S. Bebbiana* Sarg.)

This is closely related to the pussy willow and occurs frequently with it but shows a preference for drier soil. It is from six to eighteen feet high, does not spread from the root and often has the habit of a small tree with a distinct trunk. The catkins appear as distinguishing features in early spring with the leaves rather than ahead of them, as with pussy willow. The seed capsules are borne on long thread-like pedicels and taper to an especially long slender beak, which gives the distinctive name. In summer after the flowers and fruit are gone one must rely on the leaf characters described in the key, the mature leaves being dull green above, stoutly veined and soft-hairy beneath. The leaf margins vary from toothed to nearly entire. The young twigs are also minutely hairy. Owing to its wide soil adaptation, this species may well be used in planting where a willow is desired for mass effect.

PRAIRIE WILLOW. *Salix humilis* Marsh.

This is the common willow of dry, sandy barrens, rarely found elsewhere. It is two to eight feet high with leaves somewhat smaller than the last, dark green and smooth above, persistently gray-woolly below with the margins commonly more or less rolled downward or reflexed.

SHINING WILLOW.   *Salix lucida* Muhl.

The shining willow is a tall shrub or low bushy tree of six to fifteen feet, common on moist banks and roadside thickets throughout the state. It is easily recognized by its glossy or shining leaves which may flash the light as if wax-polished. These are large, (three to five by one to one and one-half inches) taper pointed, darker above but also green and shining below.   The staminate catkins are large and showy but less familiar than those of the pussy willow, partly because they are later, appearing with the leaves in early May. It deserves wide use for ornamental planting, being the most valuable of the native willows for this purpose, both on account of its beautiful lustrous foliage and its showy catkins.   For such purpose the staminate plants should be selected.   Since the sex cannot be determined in young plants, for such use, old roots should be moved or else cuttings taken from the desired plants.   Although preferring moisture it will grow in dry soil.

HEART-LEAVED WILLOW.   *Salix cordata* Muhl.

The heart-leaved willow is a tall, stout, branched shrub of five to twelve feet, with a number of varieties and hybrids. This is common with the pussy willow in low wet soils throughout Vermont. The flower catkins precede the leaves and are comparatively small and slender.   The twigs are slightly downy or smooth.   The leaves serve best to distinguish it, being long and narrow, lance-shaped, with base usually somewhat rounded or heart-shaped and margins varying from sharply toothed to nearly entire.   They are green on both sides or slightly paler beneath, the young ones often silky or downy but becoming smooth with age. The stipules are usually large and conspicuous, especially on the vigorous young shoots and help in its recognition.

PURPLE OSIER WILLOW. *Salix purpurea* L.

This is one of the favorite basket willows of the old world. It is not a native of America but was widely introduced in the eastern colonies by the early settlers. In this way it was established throughout Vermont and it has since persisted and spread in moist soil along water-courses. It is also sometimes planted for ornament. It may be recognized by its long slender purplish-green branches and its narrow smooth dark green leaves which have a blue cast above as seen in mass and are somewhat glaucous or whitish beneath. Upon drying the leaves and young twigs turn purplish black which probably suggested the name of the species. Willows of fine quality for basket making can be grown in Vermont and doubtless there will sometime be a revival of attention to this industry. Its development is primarily dependent upon local labor conditions since basket making as a winter occupation must, as a rule be combined with some summer industry. At Syracuse, N. Y., it is so associated with the salt works.

THE LESS COMMON VERMONT WILLOWS

In addition to these six common shrubby willows there are nine or ten others, all rare. These will merely be listed with brief statement as to occurrence. For descriptions, reference may be made to botanical texts. It will be noted that three of these are mountain species, that two grow in cold bogs, and that four are found on shore regions.

BALSAM WILLOW. *S. balsamifera* Barratt. A northern species known only at Mt. Mansfield, Elmore Mountain and Long Pond in Westmore.

TEA-LEAVED WILLOW. *S. phylicifolia* L. An alpine species, moist ravines, summit Mt. Mansfield.

BEAR-BERRY WILLOW. *S. Uva-ursi* Pursh. Prostrate on bleakest portions of summit, Mt. Mansfield.

BOG WILLOW. *S. pedicillaris* Pursh. Occasional in peat bogs of the Champlain valley.

HOARY WILLOW. *S. candida* Flügge. Occasional in cold bogs.

SAND-BAR WILLOW. *S. longifolia* Muhl. (*S. fluviatalis* Nutt.) Occasional on sand shores of Lake Champlain and Connecticut River.

SLENDER WILLOW. *S. petiolaris* Smith. Frequent in Lake Champlain swamps.

SILKY WILLOW. *S. sericea* Marsh. Frequent in swamps and along streams.

NORTHERN HOARY WILLOW. *Salix pellita* Anders. Only one station is known at Bloomfield.

OAK FAMILY. CUPULIFERAE

This family includes among trees, the oak, birch and chestnut, all of which are described in "Trees of Vermont." There are also two shrubby species of oak found in southern Vermont, the bear oak, (*Quercus ilicifolia* Wang.) and the scrub chestnut oak (*Q. prinoides* Willd.), reference to both of which will be found in the bulletin cited. Two other groups of shrubs are also of this family, the alders and the hazel-nuts. Their flowers appear in very early spring in separate clusters on the same plant. The staminate or pollen-bearing hang as long, pendent catkins; the pistillate or seed-producing are small and upright, looking more like buds than flowers.

THE ALDERS

There are three well-marked species of alder in Vermont with possibly a fourth. Only two of them are common but all three are included in the following key. Alder bark is rich in tannin and has also medicinal properties. It is not, however, much used in America.

KEY TO VERMONT ALDERS

1. Flowers developed in earliest spring before the leaves, leaves not sticky (glutinous). The common alders of the lower altitudes 2
1. Flowers developed in spring with the leaves, young leaves sticky (glutinous). Rare species of the mountains and cool banks.
Green alders.

2. Leaves whitish and mostly hairy or downy beneath. Usually pointed at the tip and rounded or cordate at the base.
Hoary alder.

2. Leaves green both sides, usually smooth underneath rounded at the tip and more or less wedge shaped at base..Smooth alder.

HOARY OR SPECKLED ALDER. *Alnus incana* (L.) Moench.

This is the common alder of Vermont which borders every stream and is the plague of the trout fisher.   It often forms dense shrubby thickets, while individual specimens may show the habit of small trees twenty feet high.   The leaf and cone-like fruit are well shown in the fig-

HOARY ALDER.
Leaf and fruit, × ½.

ure. The leaves often vary, and a fungus may cause some of the scales of the cones to develop numerous curled, tongue-like outgrowths, often an inch long. Very little use is made of the alder in Vermont, although where large enough it makes excellent fuel.   Formerly the charcoal burners used it, making an unusually good product from it.   In Japan where it attains a height of sixty feet or more it furnishes valuable wood. While at first thought this would be rated a plant of little or no value, it doubtless proves more serviceable than is any other plant or shrub as a means of preventing the banks of streams from washing away.   If nature did not plant it, the land owners would probably have to provide some substitute as a soil binder.

SMOOTH ALDER.   *Alnus rugosa* (Du Roi) Spreng.   (*A. serrulata* Willd.)

The smooth alder is the common species from Massachusetts southward and naturally is more common in southern

Vermont than northward.   In general character and habit it is almost like the preceding.   In well-marked forms it is easy to distinguish the two by the leaves. It should be noted, however, that an intermediate form often occurring along the shores of Lake Champlain puzzles the student.   The leaf of this form has the shape of the hoary and the color of the smooth alder.   It is listed as a hybrid in the "Flora of Vermont"; but whether or not this is the true explanation must be determined by further study.

SMOOTH ALDER, × ½.

THE GREEN ALDERS

There are two rarer northern species easily distinguishable from the preceding by their smaller rounder leaves which are distinctly glutinous especially on the under side.   It is also an interesting fact that the fruit of these green alders seems free from the gall fungus.   The typical green alder (*A. crispa* (Ait.) Pursh., *A. viridis* DC.) is found only on the higher mountain summits.   It is a small shrub of from two to six feet.   The larger form of lower altitudes which may rival the common alder in size has recently been described as a distinct species (*A. mollis* Fernald).   It is distinguished from the mountain species by more pubescent shoots and lower leaf surfaces.

HAZELNUTS

There are two species of hazelnuts in Vermont. Only one, the beaked hazel, is common, and there is scarcely enough of this except in some of the higher mountain pastures to tempt boys to harvest the nuts. Further west and south the larger American hazelnut is more common and is gathered in quantity by country children. In Europe a related species, the European hazel (*Corylus avellana*) has been improved and brought into culture, furnishing the familiar filbert-nut of commerce. Sometimes the hazelnut is confused with the witch-hazel described later in this pamphlet. There is no occasion for this, however, other than the name. The two hazelnuts are readily distinguishable by the fruits as follows:

Husks (involucral bracts) united and prolonged into a long tubular
    beak, about twice the length of the nut......Beaked hazelnut.
Husks nearly distinct and not prolonged into a beak.
                                        American hazelnut.

BEAKED HAZELNUT. *Corylus rostrata* Ait.

This is the common hazelnut of Vermont, frequent in dry wayside thickets throughout the state. It is a small shrub,

BEAKED HAZELNUT.
Leaf and fruit, × ½.

usually of three to five feet, with stems small and clustered owing to a tendency to throw up suckers from the base.   The shape of leaf and fruit are well shown in the accompanying cut. The leaf is usually two to three inches long, and rather harsh to the touch.   The flowers appear before the leaves in earliest spring.   The staminate or pollen-bearing are in graceful drooping catkins; the pistillate ones, from which the nuts are to develop, are smaller, budlike and scarcely noticeable except for the bright red stigmas protruding from the scales.   The bracts rapidly enlarge in early summer and show the beaked character, but the nuts do not mature till autumn.

AMERICAN HAZELNUT.   *Corylus americana* Walt.

This is naturally a more southern plant than the preceding, thriving at its best in the warmer, longer summers found

AMERICAN HAZELNUT, × ½.

southward and westward. The shrub is taller and the nut somewhat larger than that of the other species.   The nut varies much in quality and size, the best being nearly as large as the ordinary market filberts and of quite as agreeable flavor. Without doubt the best of these will some day be brought into culture and probably improved as the European species has been.

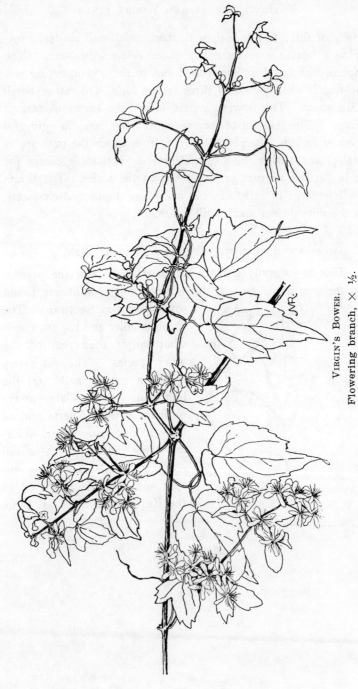

VIRGIN'S BOWER.
Flowering branch, × ½.

CROWFOOT FAMILY. RANUNCULACEAE

Herbs like the common buttercups and anemones are more typical of this family than are the woody members. Two species of clematis, the most attractive of Vermont's flowering vines, are the only representatives of the latter class. Both have slender, weak stems, somewhat woody below, and climb by the strong leaf-stalks which clasp any available support. The foliage and flowers are graceful and the fruit scarcely less so, making these the most dainty of our native vines, whether in their natural habitats or when brought into culture. The two species may be distinguished as follows:

Flowers small (one-half to one inch), white, in leafy clusters.
Virgin's bower.

Flowers large (two to four inches), purple and solitary.
Purple clematis.

VIRGIN'S BOWER. *Clematis virginiana* L.

This is a familiar sight fringing streams and moist thickets, soon converting the ugliest spot into a place of beauty. Its compound leaves have each three leaflets with clasping petioles. The plants are dioecious, that is, some have only pollen-bearing flowers and others only seed-producing ones. The fruits are provided with long feathery tails and as they ripen in autumn are almost as showy as the flowers. If one is selecting vines for ornamental planting, he should aim to secure a good proportion of these fruitful plants.

PURPLE CLEMATIS. *Clematis verticillaris* DC.

This is a rather rare plant on rocky hills. It is a weaker climber and less luxuriant than is the other species, hence is somewhat less desirable as a screen or fence-cover. Its strikingly beautiful flowers however compensate for this weaker and less luxuriant habit of growth and make it one of the peculiarly attractive native ornamental vines. Its fruits have feathery appendages like the virgin's bower, giving it a charm in autumn as well as in spring.

BARBERRY FAMILY.　BERBERIDACEAE

COMMON BARBERRY.　*Berberis vulgaris* L.

There are no native plants of this family but the common barberry, originally introduced from Europe, has now become so frequent an escape by roadsides and in waste places as often to appear as if native.　It is a shrub of six to eight feet with thorny branches and bristly leaves.　The younger branches have a gracefully arching habit and produce in late spring an abundance of small yellow flowers in drooping clusters followed by masses of fruit which redden beautifully in autumn and persist through the winter.　It will grow well on even the thinnest of

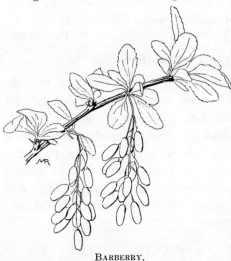

BARBERRY.
Fruiting branch, × ½.

soils. It also bears pruning at will.　These characters combine to make it one of the most valuable of shrubs for ornamental planting, especially for hedges or close groups to exclude trespassers. The berries though tart are edible and throughout New England are employed in the concoction of preserves, particularly in combination with fruits of milder quality, like the apple. They are sometimes put in cucumber pickles. No other use is made of the plant here, we believe, but the barberry has been used from ancient times for medicine and dye and for tanning leather. The tannin occurs in the bark. A yellow coloring matter is found in the bark, more especially in that of the root, the extract from which can be used for dyeing cloth or leather.

MOONSEED FAMILY. MENISPERMACEAE

MOONSEED. *Menispermum canadense* L.

The moonseed is the only native representative of its family. It is a slender, perennial, twining vine, somewhat woody below but herbaceous above, which occurs occasionally climbing over shrubs on the banks of streams and in low thickets.   It is

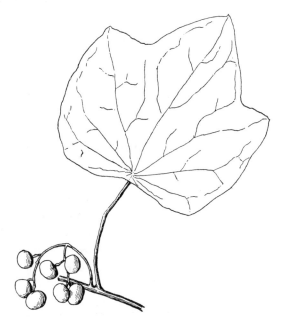

MOONSEED, × ½.

easily recognized by its leaf which is rather large, four to six inches across, of unusual shape and veining as shown in the drawing, the petiole is attached just within the margin and the under side is paler and strongly veined. The flowers and fruits are rather inconspicuous. This is sometimes used for ornamental planting and the roots are reputed to possess medicinal virtues.

LAUREL FAMILY. LAURACEAE

This family takes its name from the laurel or bay-tree of Europe, the leaves of which were the emblem of victory. The name laurel is commonly applied in this country to certain

shrubs of the heath family, the mountain laurel and sheep laurel to be described later. The only members we have of the laurel family properly speaking, however, are the sassafras and spice-bush. The former is a small tree common from Massachusetts southward. It is at its northern limit in southern Vermont where it occurs but sparingly. It does not often reach the stature of a tree in this state but nevertheless it was described in "Trees of Vermont." We will simply reproduce the plate

SASSAFRAS

Leaves and young fruit, × ⅛

here showing the peculiar leaf outline and refer to that bulletin for further description. The medicinal qualities of sassafras have long been celebrated.

SPICE-BUSH. FEVER-BUSH. *Benzoin aestivale* (L.) Nees. (*Lindera benzoin* Blume.)

This is a rare plant in Vermont found in the shade of moist woods and along streams. It is a shrub of four to six feet with slender twigs and graceful habit. The flowers are small and yellow appearing in nearly sessile clusters in early spring ahead

of the leaves. The leaves are alternate, two to five inches long, with entire margins, paler beneath, smooth or rarely downy. The botanical name was suggested by the strong aromatic odor resembling gum-benzoin, which resides in all parts of the plant. This shrub is worthy of ornamental planting, doing best in shaded situations. An infusion of the bark is sometimes used as a tonic and stimulant, especially in intermittent fevers and the leaves served the southerners as a substitute for tea during the civil war. In revolutionary times the powdered fruits were used in place of allspice.

Spice Bush, × ½.

SAXIFRAGE FAMILY. SAXIFRAGACEAE

This family includes only the one genus of woody plants, the others being the herbaceous saxifrages and mitreworts.

CURRANTS AND GOOSEBERRIES

Vermont has three native species each of the currant and of the gooseberry. They all have leaves so similar as to suggest the family relationship: they are simple, palmately veined and lobed and usually borne in small clusters. The fruit also is characteristic. Where the species is unknown the following key will aid in its recognition:

1. Stems usually bearing thorns at the base of leaf stalks or leaf clusters and often with scattered bristly prickles; berries prickly or smooth. (Gooseberries) 2
1. Stems without thorns or prickles. (Currants)...............4
2. Flowers several (a raceme) on a nodding stem, twigs and fruit bristly ....Swamp gooseberry.

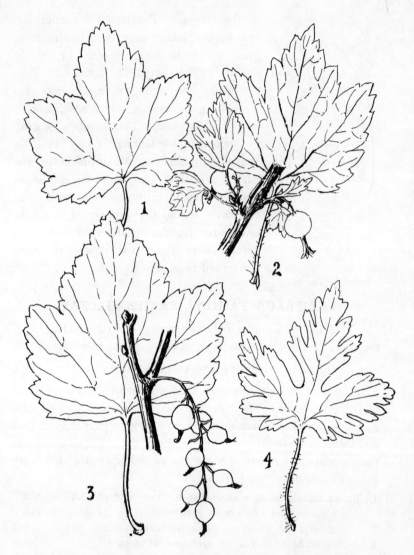

1, MOUNTAIN CURRANT;   3, SWAMP RED CURRANT;

2, SMOOTH GOOSEBERRY;   4, SWAMP GOOSEBERRY.

Natural size.

2. Flowers in clusters of one to three, stems without thorns or
     bristles except at base of leaves 3
3. Flower stems short (about one-half incl.), fruit smooth.
                                          Smooth gooseberry.
3. Flower stem one inch or more, fruit usually with prickles.
                                          Prickly gooseberry.
4. Flower clusters erect, berries bristly..........Mountain currant.
4. Flower cluster drooping, berries smooth 5
5. Flowers large, bell-shaped, whitish; berries black when ripe.
                                          Black currant.
5. Flowers small, flat, greenish; berries red when ripe..Red currant.

THE GOOSEBERRIES

A considerable use was made by the early settlers of the
fruit of the wild gooseberries. That of the swamp gooseberry
is small and unpleasant, but both of the others are good.   In
England the wild gooseberry is inferior to these, yet from it by
culture and improvement they have produced cultivated fruits
which are very productive with berries as large as small plums.
These European gooseberries are liable to mildew and are not
fully hardy in Vermont, hence we must depend on American types.
The gooseberries commonly seen in Vermont gardens originated
from the American smooth gooseberry.   Both this and the
prickly berry offer promising opportunity for further breeding,
selection and improvement.

SMOOTH GOOSEBERRY. *Ribes oxyacanthoides* L.

This is frequent in cold wet woods and swamps throughout
Vermont. It is a spreading shrub a few feet in height, with slender branches and thorns at base of leaf clusters short and sometimes lacking. The shape of the leaves is shown in the drawing. They are thin and finely pubescent below, three to five
lobed and toothed. The flowers are on short stalks, bell-shaped.
The fruit is a smooth globular berry, one-third to one-half inch
in diameter, either green or reddish when ripe and delicious in
preserves or jam. This is the parent of the cultivated American
gooseberries like Houghton and Downing.

PRICKLY GOOSEBERRY. *Ribes Cynosbati* L.

This is the common gooseberry of rocky woods. It generally has slender pointed thorns at the base of the leaf cluster and often the branches have scattered prickles in addition. The

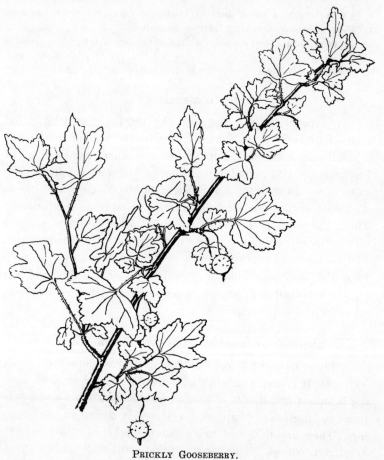

PRICKLY GOOSEBERRY.
Fruiting branch, × ½.

leaves are usually roundish heart-shaped at the base and slightly downy beneath and on the stem. The berries are one-third to one-half inch in diameter, armed with long prickles or rarely smooth, ripening to a dull purple. It is sweet and edible, not infrequently cultivated and well worthy of further trial and improvement.

SWAMP GOOSEBERRY. *Ribes lacustre* (Pers.) Poir.

This is frequent in cold swamps and wet mountain woods. It is an upright shrub of three to four feet, the young stems clothed with bristles. The leaves are heart-shaped at the base and deeply three to five lobed, this deep lobing distinguishing it from any of the other species. The purplish flowers are open bell-shaped. The berries are reddish, covered with weak bristles, very small (one-sixth inch) and of unpleasant flavor. The only use ever made of this is for ornamental planting in wet soils.

THE CURRANTS.

RED CURRANT. *Ribes triste* Pall. var *albinervium* (Mx.) Fern.
(*R. rubrum* L. var. *subglandulosum* Maxim.)

The cultivated red and white garden currants are descended from the European red currant known as *Ribes vulgare*. Our native American variety differs but slightly therefrom except in habit. It is occasionally found in cold damp woods or bogs. Its general characters so closely resemble those of the familiar garden currants that description here is needless. The berries are smaller than the garden varieties, bright red and edible.

The natural growth of this wild currant in cold, wet woods explains why the cultivated currants do so well in cool moist soil, with abundant fertility, and have preference for northern exposures or even partial shade.

BLACK CURRANT. *Ribes floridum* L'Her.

The black currant is a more or less erect shrub found scattered in woodlands. The conspicuous drooping clusters of flowers followed by the rather large black berries render it easy of recognition. If one is in doubt however, a distinguishing mark may be found in the tiny, yellowish resinous dots sprinkled over the leaf surface, barely seen with the naked eye but clearly evident with a magnifying glass. This currant is sometimes transferred to garden culture and is a fruit of some present value and of much promise when attention may be given to its improvement. It is closely related to the European black currant which is prized by foreigners as a garden fruit.

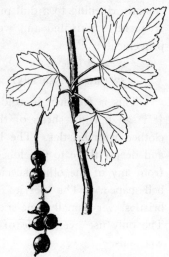

BLACK CURRANT, × ½.

MOUNTAIN CURRANT. *Ribes prostratum* L'Her.

This also goes under the names of skunk currant or fetid currant, which well characterize it since the bruised fruit and, to a less degree, the foliage emit an unpleasant odor, much like the skunk cabbage. The name mountain currant is also well applied since it is one of the common and characteristic shrubs of the higher mountain woods. The Latin name was chosen because of the reclining habit of the main stems which lie along the ground and frequently root, sending up shorter erect branches. The fruit is small, bristly and of such disagreeable flavor as to preclude any use being made of it.

WITCH-HAZEL FAMILY. HAMAMELIDAE

This family includes the liquidambar or sweet-gum tree of the South but in Vermont is represented by the witch-hazel only.

WITCH-HAZEL. *Hamamelis virginiana* L.

It is a rather curious fact, and somewhat of a reproach to current methods of education, that there are probably a score of people who are acquainted with witch-hazel extract for one who is familiar with the witch-hazel plant, even in those sections of Vermont where it is common. It is a tall bushy shrub of five to fifteen feet or sometimes a small tree of twenty feet or more, with long forking brown branches. The leaves are rather large and of easily recognizable shape with wavy margin and oblique base as shown in the figure. The flower and fruit both have unusual and interesting characters. Witch-hazel is unique among our shrubs in that it blossoms in very late autumn.

WITCH-HAZEL.
Flowering in autumn, × ½.

What is more cheering after the early frosts than to come upon this shrub already leafless but with branches fringed with delicate yellow blossoms prophetic of the return of spring? The flowers are thus fertilized in the autumn, but the fruit does not enlarge until the next season, when the downy, nut-like, oval capsules become about one-half inch or more long and in the early autumn split elastically at the end in such a way as to shoot to some distance the rather large glossy-black seeds. On a sunny autumn day these may be heard snapping like toy pistols in the wayside thickets. A few branches with unopened fruit placed in the school room will illustrate in a convincing manner the effectiveness of nature's provision for seed dissemination. Witch-hazel has value as a shrub for ornamental planting because of its compact habit, clean bright foliage and autumnal flowers. Witch-hazel extract is familiar as a mildly soothing lotion. It is made by pounding or chopping the bark of the young twigs and roots and extracting, either with water, as the American Indians did, or with alcohol as prescribed by the modern pharmacopaea. The forked branches of the witch-hazel were formerly much used as "divining rods" in searching for hidden springs of water or deposits of ore, a use reflected in its common name.

ROSE FAMILY. ROSACEAE [1]

This is the most numerous family of native shrubs as well as the most useful. More than forty species and varieties are listed in the following pages and it is to be remembered in justice to the family's importance that it includes in addition a dozen or more native trees and a much larger number of herbaceous plants. The rose family has given us nearly all of the finest fruits of the temperate zone as well as the favorites among the woody ornamental plants. One needs only a partial list to realize the value to man of this one family. It includes among the fruits, the apple, pear, quince, peach, plum, cherry, almond, raspberry, blackberry, strawberry. Among the ornamentals are the rose, hawthorn, spiraea, nine-bark, flowering quinces and almonds; and to this list might be added an indefinitely long list of lesser importance. The value of these plants economically is much enhanced by their variability. In the rose family we frequently find nature in the process of species making, that is to say the plants are in a variable or plastic state, not yet stable and finished products. This gives the horticulturist his opportunity to select and shape at pleasure, as we see in the countless varieties of the rosaceous flowers and fruits listed above, many of them (e. g. all the apples) derived from a single species. But for the botanist of classical type who is happy in proportion to the exactness of his system of classification, this family offers problems at every turn. The common roses and blackberries may puzzle even an expert and the

---

[1] Mr. W. W. Eggleston carefully edited this account of the rose family and prepared the descriptions and keys in the more critical genera, including the blackberry-raspberry group (*Rubus*) the rose, the thornapple and the shad-bush.

relationships among the thorn apples in a single rocky pasture may present questions impossible of satisfactory answer at present.   While every beginner in botany should early make the acquaintance of the rose family, it need not discourage him, or even the most advanced student, if forms are found which depart from the accepted descriptions of species.

With this warning, an attempt is here made to reduce the characterization of the commoner shrubby species to such simple terms as well suffice for their recognition:

KEY TO GENERA OF ROSACEOUS SHRUBS.

1. Pistil single, maturing into a single cherry-like fruit....Cherries.
1. Pistils several, fruit not cherry-like 2
2. Leaves simple 3
2. Leaves compound 4
3. Fruit inconspicuous and dry ....Hardhacks.
3. Fruit conspicuous, fleshy 5
4. Fruit inconspicuous and dry ....Cinquefoil.
4. Fruit conspicuous, fleshy (blackberry and raspberry)......Rubus.
4. Fruit conspicuous, a rose hip ....Roses.
5. Seeds with hard, bony covering ....Thorn apples.
5. Seeds with thin, membraneceous covering 6
6. Fruit black, flesh puckery and dry ....Chokeberries.
6. Fruit red, sweet and juicy ....Serviceberries.

CHERRIES.

There are seven species of cherries and one plum spontaneous in Vermont, aside from the numerous garden varieties. The plum and five of the cherries were included in bulletin 73, "Trees of Vermont."   One kind, the choke-cherry, discussed in the former bulletin, is better described as a shrub but since it was there described and is so familiar a plant it will simply be figured here.   The wild red cherry also has often a habit as well termed shrubby as tree-like but that too was described in the tree bulletin and so will here be omitted.   There are, however

CHOKE CHERRY.
Leaves, flowers and fruit, × ¼.

WILD RED CHERRY.
Leaves, flowers and fruit, × ⅛.

(From Trees of Vermont).

the two dwarf sand cherries, characterized by low shrubby habit and other characters as follows:

Older stems trailing ....Sand cherry.
Stems upright ....Appalachian cherry.

SAND CHERRY. *Prunus pumila* L.

The sand cherry occurs occasionally in Vermont, usually on rocky or sandy banks of streams. The main stems are semi-

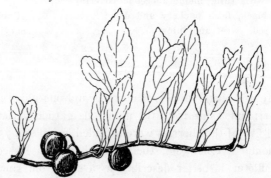

SAND CHERRY, × ⅔.

prostrate, the younger branches more or less erect, sometimes a foot or two in height. The leaves are quite long and narrow, tapering to base and apex, sharp pointed and sharply toothed toward the apex. The fruit is a small, dark red cherry, nearly black when ripe, one-third to one-half inch in diameter, with flesh thin, acid and rather astringent, scarcely edible. This is sometimes planted in parks to cover rocky banks.

APPALACHIAN CHERRY. *Prunus cuneata* Raf.

This differs from the preceding in uprightness of habit, in larger flowers and in leaf relatively shorter and broader with a more rounded apex. It has been found in Vermont in only a few places on sandy soils in the vicinity of Burlington.

HARDHACK. SPIRAEA.

This name "hardhack" is applied rather loosely to several plants in Vermont, but to most New England farmers it suggests the commonest of the shrubby pasture weeds, also known as steeple-bush. There are two native species of spiraea growing intermingled and scarcely distinguished in the popular mind. Both come under the opprobrious name of hardhack, so that for differentiation in Vermont the names steeple-bush and meadow-sweet serve best. The Siberian spiraea (*Sorbaria sorbifolia*) with its large showy panicles of white flowers and mountain-ash-like leaves is frequent about old gardens and will probably be recognized in most cases without a key. The two native species may be at once distinguished as follows:

Young shoots and lower leaf surfaces rusty downy.......Steeple-bush.
Shoots and leaves nearly or quite smooth.............Meadow sweet.

STEEPLE-BUSH.   *Spiraea tomentosa* L.

This is so familiar that reference to the illustration, to avoid possible error in usage of the name, is all that is needed. Every Vermonter knows its characteristics. Wherever there is a neglected wayside or pasture, especially in the moister spots,

the steeple bush soon raises its spire-like flower clusters.   When in fresh bloom its delicate rose tints contrasting with the dark green foliage are pleasing to one who can forget its weedy aggressiveness.   A few years ago the alarming increase of this shrub in rocky pastures, formerly so pro- ductive, was a cause of much regret to thrifty farmers.   Today it is realized that the hard-hack spires are often an emblem of hope, pointing to the better days soon to come when, under wise encouragement, nature is to reforest these rocky lands with spruce and pine, the noblest and most profitable crops that can be grown upon them.   Darlington says that the steeple- bush was, on account of its astrin- gency, formerly considerably used in do- mestic medicines in New England.   Its

STEEPLE-BUSH.

In flower, × ½.

day as a medicine is probably largely past, but it is so attractive a shrub that it is sure to become more valued for use in ornamental planting.   It is sometimes called woolly spiraea in contrast with the species figured and described on the opposite page.

MEADOW SWEET. *Spiraea latifolia* Borkh. L. (*S. salicifolia* L. of earlier botanies.)

This is also termed the smooth spiraea; sometimes still more complimentary names are given it,—quaker-lady and queen-of the meadow. The farmers, even, will use a softer name than for the other, since this stays closer by swamps and wet ground less valued for pasture. It is somewhat taller and more branching than the preceding with larger and more open cluster of white or pinkish flowers. It is less striking but more delicate than the steeple-bush for landscape effects.

Introduced species. There are a large number of shrubby spiraeas which are hardy in this climate and offered for sale by nurserymen. The bridal wreath (*Spiraea Van Houttei*) is the most showy of these and frequent in cultivation. Others which are often planted are *Spiraea Japonica* (or *callosa*)

Flowering stem, X ½.

MEADOW-SWEET.

S. prunifolia and *S. Thunbergii.* All have come from Asiatic ancestors.

CHOKEBERRY. *Pyrus arbutifolia* (L.) L. f.

There are two species of the chokeberry in Vermont. Blanchard has found in Windham county the typical red chokeberry (*Pyrus arbutifolia*) with quite showy red fruits which may adorn the branches even through the winter. The common

CHOKEBERRY, × ½.

plant in swamps, throughout the state is the

BLACK CHOKEBERRY. *Pyrus melanocarpa* (Mx.) Willd.

This is a shrub generally three to six feet high but may exceed that size. In general characters it is like the preceding species with upright habit and dark green rather handsome foliage. The leaves of this species are nearly smooth throughout, whereas the other is hairy below. The fruit in this black chokeberry is larger (one-fourth to one-third of an inch) in diameter and of shining black color. The berries are sweetish but too astringent to permit eating and no use is made of this shrub except for its sparing use in ornamental planting. Occasionally, either by mistake or otherwise, the berries are collected and sold as a huckleberry.

SERVICE-BERRY. AMELANCHIER.

The common June-berry or shad, often called sugar-plum, is typically a tree and treated in "Trees of Vermont." As there stated it ranges in size from a small tree to a shrub so the cut from that bulletin is here reproduced. The shrubby varieties and species resemble it in their abundance of white blossoms in early spring, with sweet edible red or purple berries, ripening in June or early July. All of the service berries produce attractive fruits which are promptly eaten by the birds. It seems possible that by selection and culture varieties desirable for the fruit garden may some day be produced.

SERVICEBERRY.
Leaves, flowers and fruit, × ⅓.
(From Trees of Vermont, p. 68).

Two things — aside from their small size— which preclude more general use of the wild berries at present are their irregularity in time of ripening and the promptness of the birds in harvesting them. The shrubby shad-bushes may be distinguished by the following characters:

1. Flowers 1-4, leaves acute at base, fruit pear-shaped or ellipsoidal
                                        Mountain shadbush.
1. Flowers 5 to many, leaves obtuse or cordate at base, fruit
    globose 2
2. Leaves finely serrate or entire, flowers early in May.
                                        Early or rock shadbush.
2. Leaves coarsely serrate, flowers 2 weeks or more later.
                                        Late or shore shadbush.

ROCK SHAD-BUSH. *Amelanchier oblongifolia* (T. & G.) Roem.

This species is more commonly found as a small low shrub in rocky woods, although it sometimes occurs several feet high. The young leaves and racemes are densely white hairy; the leaves are oblong, rounded at the ends; and the fruit is ripe in June and July.

SHORE SHAD-BUSH. *Amelanchier spicata* (Lam.) Koch. (*A. rotundifolia* Roem.)

This shrub is sometimes 10 or 12 feet high and is of more northern range than is the last. It is commonly found on rocky shores. This is the late-flowering and fruiting shad, with coarsely toothed leaves. It fruits from August to September.

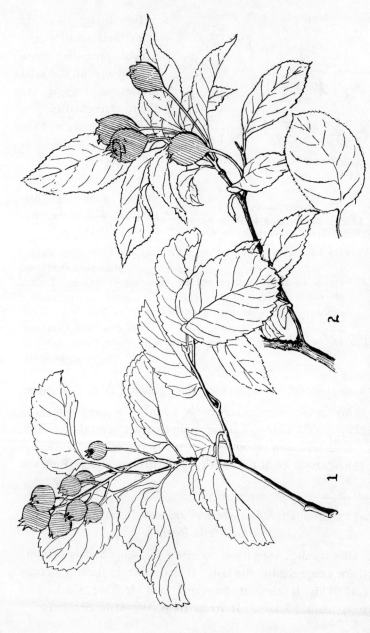

1, Shore Shadbush; 2, Mountain Shadbush, × ⅔. The unnumbered leaf in the lower right hand corner is that of the Rock Shadbush.

MOUNTAIN SHAD-BUSH. *Amelanchier oligocarpa* (Michx.) Roem.

This is the common shad-bush of the higher altitudes of the Green Mountains and is easily distinguished by the few flowers, the pear-shaped larger fruit and the acute leaves.

A form, *A. arguta* Nutt., with ellipsoidal fruit and smaller leaves is found occasionally in the lowland swamps.

The fruits of these species are less desirable than those of the previously named species.

CINQUEFOIL. POTENTILLA.

The cinquefoils or five-fingers are mostly herbaceous weeds. Two shrubby species occur in Vermont, however, one of them becoming rather too familiar in some sections. They are plants of quite different type as shown by the following characters:

Height 2 to 4 feet; compound leaf of 5 to 7 leaflets; flowers yellow ....Shrubby cinquefoil

Height 6 inches or less; leaf compounded of 3 leaflets; flowers white ....Three-toothed cinquefoil.

SHRUBBY CINQUEFOIL.[1] *Potentilla fruticosa.* L.

This is a low, much-branched, spreading bush, with bark scaling from the older stems, leaves a grayish green from the coating of silky hairs, and abundant conspicuous yellow flowers as bright and nearly as large as buttercup blossoms. It was originally found only occasionally bordering swamps and in a few cool, rocky gorges or cliffs. During the last generation however, it has been spreading persistently over the pastures in certain sections until today it must be ranked as the most aggressive invader among the shrubby weeds, quite outclassing the hardhacks. It is worst in the vicinity of Manchester and Dorset but extends northward to Salisbury and southward along the

---

[1] For a detailed account of the shrubby cinquefoil as a weed in Vermont, see Vt. Sta. Rpt. 16, p. 173 (1903).

Taconic range, through Massachusetts and Connecticut. It is difficult to understand why it is less aggressive elsewhere unless it be because of its preference for lime which abounds in the sec-

tion indicated. Plowing and close pasturing have been used successfully to check its progress. There is apparently so extreme an antipathy between this plant and the butternut that wherever the butternut tree gets started the shrub must perish. This suggests the possibility of exterminating the cinquefoil by planting butternuts. Reforestation of any kind, however, will soon suppress it. Wherever it has not

SHRUBBY CINQUEFOIL, × ½.

become a serious pest farmers should take warning and keep it out. It has been given a variety of local names, Manchester weed, prairie-weed, yellow hardhack, sage-brush, etc. This shrub occurs also in Europe and it may surprise some farmers who have too much of it to know that as introduced from Europe through the nursery trade it has been rather frequently sold in Vermont for ornamental planting. It is an attractive shrub and there is no evidence that it has ever spread in such cases.

THREE-TOOTHED CINQUEFOIL. *Potentilla tridentata* Ait.

This is a rather rare plant found along the rocky summits of several of the Vermont mountains and higher foothills. It has a shrubby base but the shoots never rise more than a few inches. Each of the leaflets ends in three teeth, whence the name. The white flowers, less than one-half inch across, are borne in a rather pretty small terminal cluster. It is an attractive plant for use in rockeries.

RASPBERRY, BLACKBERRY AND DEWBERRY.   RUBUS.

The raspberries and blackberries supply some of the finest and most abundant of the wild fruit of Vermont. These with the dewberries belong to the genus *Rubus*. It will conduce to clearness sharply to segregate in one's mind the members of the two fundamental groups of this genus as follows:

The thimble-shaped fruit or "berry" separable from the receptacle or "core" when ripe ....Raspberries.
The fruit or "berry" firmly attached to the end of the fruit stem or receptacle which remains as a "core" in the mature fruit.
Blackberries and dewberries.
(See key to these, page 108).

RASPBERRIES.

1. Leaves simple, flowers large, rose-like in color and form.
Flowering raspberry.
1. Leaves compound, flowers smaller, white 2
2. Fruit red, stems bristly, without whitish bloom, stoloniferous
    (i. e. spreading by underground stems) ....Red raspberry.
2. Fruit black, stems prickly, with whitish bloom (glaucous), root-
    ing at apex ....Black raspberry.

These three species of raspberry are so well known and easily distinguishable as to call for an apology for the insertion of the above key, except for two matters which contribute to confusion of ideas. The first is the popular misuse of the name "mulberry" for the flowering rasberry in Vermont. It is to be hoped that this publication may contribute to the cor-- rect usage of these words. The second is, that where the black and red raspberries grow intermingled, they may hybridize. As a result the berry picker occasionally finds a "purple-cane berry" which is neither red nor black, but clearly a cross be- tween the two. This species, *Rubus neglectus* of the botanies, has the stem, branches and tipping habit of the black raspberry, with prickles of the red raspberry, and purplish red fruit which is firmer than the red raspberry and has something of the black raspberry taste. In the garden several improved forms of this are in cultivation e. g. the Shaffer.

FLOWERING RASPBERRY.   Blossom and young fruit, × ½.

On the limestone ledges of Cavendish there occurs an interesting native form of the European raspberry, (*Rubus idaeus* L. var. *anomalus* Arrh.)

The red dewberry is sometimes mistakenly called dwarf raspberry, but is here placed with the dewberries where it more properly belongs.

FLOWERING RASPBERRY. *Rubus odoratus* L.

The flowering raspberry is also known as thimbleberry and erroneously as "mulberry." The true mulberry is a tree and occurs native in Vermont only very rarely in Pownal. The flowering raspberry is easily distinguishable from all of the others by its large purple flowers, maple-like leaves, and its very broad fruit. The fruit is used but little, although it is edible and some people are fond of it. It is well worthy of a place in the hardy shrubbery used for ornamental purposes, but has been thus utilized but little as yet in Vermont although listed in horticultural catalogues.

RED RASPBERRY. *Rubus strigosus* Mx.

The red raspberry is abundant all over the state, but one needs to visit a recent mountain clearing to find the fruit in perfection as to size and flavor. In contrast with the black, the red raspberry is stoloniferous, that is it sends creeping underground stems from the parent plant in all directions and thus quickly forms its characteristic thickets in woodland clearings. However, this raspberry needs no introduction to a Vermonter. Great quantities of the wild fruit are annually picked in the state, and we have no more delicious fruit whether fresh or preserved. For home canning it is especially popular since no native berry keeps the natural flavor so well as the red raspberry. One of the "goodies," the compounding of which is in danger of becoming a lost art in Vermont, is the red raspberries dried with maple sugar. This confection, as well as sweet flag preserved in maple sugar were hard things for the Vermont mother of the last generation to keep hidden in the house when her boys were at home.

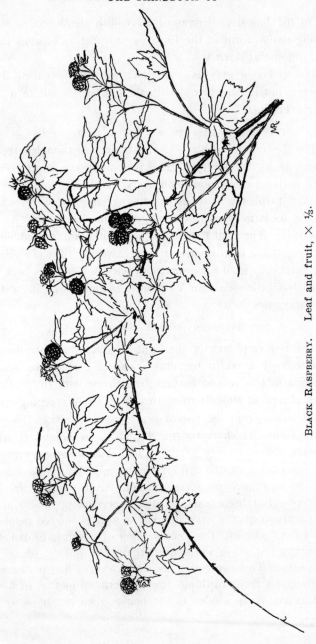

BLACK RASPBERRY.   Leaf and fruit, × ⅓.

BLACK RASPBERRY. *Rubus occidentalis* L.

This is found in the lower altitudes but never as abundantly as is the red raspberry. It always occurs in separate clusters
or "bushes," while the red raspberry, as explained above, usually
forms colonies of indefinite size. The plants are often in proximity, however, partly due to the fact that they tend to reproduce themselves fully as much by rooting at the tips as by seed.
The long arching canes are very graceful.

BLACKBERRIES AND DEWBERRIES.

This group is especially to be commended to the systematic
botanist who is seeking problems.[1] Of course everyone recognizes a blackberry bush at sight, and most would be sure of it
upon contact even in the dark; but it requires an expert botanist
to identify all of the so-called species of blackberries found in
Vermont. About a dozen of those listed in the Gray's New
Manual of Botany occur here, several of which have been so
recently described that their distribution and botanical status
are matters of doubt. Unquestionably some of these are hybrids between the older and more well marked species. It will
be necessary to await continued observation of these doubtful
forms, and probably to grow them from seed and to study their
behavior in successive generations, before the final word is said
as to their traits as well as regards their status. Herein lie
problems in the solution of which local students may participate.
With these facts in mind the writers have selected only the following common and clearly marked species for detailed con-
sideration.

---

[1]One who is trying to acquaint himself with the details of the Vermont blackberry problems from the standpoint of systematic botany,
should first consult Gray's New Manual of Botany. Both Mr. W. H.
Blanchard of Westminster and Dr. Ezra Brainerd of Middlebury have
done much work on our Vermont blackberries, and either one will
freely answer inquiries, identify specimens, or direct to the further
literature of this group.

BLACKBERRY-DEWBERRY KEY.

1. Fruit bright red when ripe, stem trailing, only slightly woody.
                                                    Red dewberry.
1. Fruit black or reddish black when ripe, stem woody............2
2. Canes erect or ascending, with the longer canes often recurved..5
2. Canes trailing 3

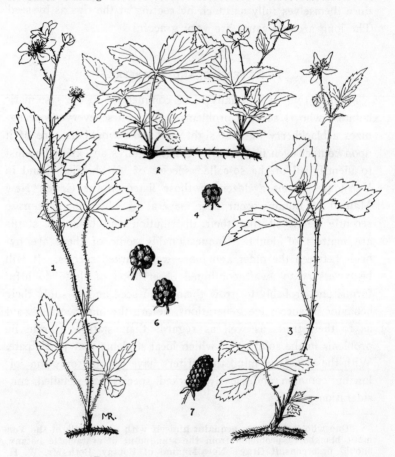

DEWBERRIES AND BLACKBERRIES, × ½.

Flowering branches: 1, Swamp Dewberry; 2, Black Dewberry; 3,
    Bristly Dewberry (*R. setosus*). Fruits: 4, Swamp Dewberry; 5,
    Black Dewberry; 6, Mountain Blackberry; 7, Highbush Blackberry.

3. Stalks (pedicels) of flowers and fruit unarmed................4
3. Stalks of flowers and fruit armed with sharp bristle-like prickles.
Bristly dewberry.

4. Fruit small, reddish-black; leaflets three, thick shining.
Swamp dewberry.

4. Fruit larger, black; leaflets 3 to 5, larger, thin, dull.
Black dewberry.

5. Stems (pedicels) of flowers and fruit covered with glandular
   hairs ....Highbush blackberry.
5. Stems of flowers and fruit glandless 6
6. Canes armed, recurved, often rooting at tips; lower surface of
   leaves downy ....Recurved blackberry.
6. Canes usually unarmed, erect; lower surface usually smooth.
Mountain blackberry.

HIGH-BUSH BLACKBERRY.   Fruiting branch, × ⅓.

HIGH-BUSH BLACKBERRY. *Rubus allegheniensis* Porter (*R. nigrobaccus* Bailey.)

This is the common blackberry to most Vermonters, especially prevalent at lower altitudes. Like the red raspberry it is at its best in a new clearing where its tall sharply armed canes make impenetrable thickets. It requires a constant supply of moisture and partial shade for its finest development; and no fruit suffers worse if a drought occurs after the berries are set. Those who are used to the sweet, juicy, spicy, long-tapering wild blackberry of the new clearings feel poorly served by the sour, seedy market berry. Surely there is still plenty of work for the horticulturist among the blackberries.

RECURVED BLACKBERRY. *Rubus recurvans* Blanchard.

This is frequently found and easily recognized by its recurved stems, often rooting at the tip. The fruit is rather short with numerous large, juicy drupelets.

MOUNTAIN BLACKBERRY. *Rubus canadensis* L.

The mountain blackberry is the common berry of the higher altitudes (above 1500 ft.) and is even a more vigorous grower than the highbush blackberry of the lower valleys. It is easily distinguished from the latter by its usually smooth canes and smooth leaflets, shorter, sour berries with large drupelets borne in short clusters.

Another blackberry, *Rubus elegantulus* Blanchard, closely allied to the above has slender prickles on the angles of the canes, rather small leaflets in threes, and slender flower clusters.

RED DEWBERRY. *Rubus triflorus* Richard.

This is frequently known as running raspberry and is a very
common trailer in our cold swamps and mountain woods. It is

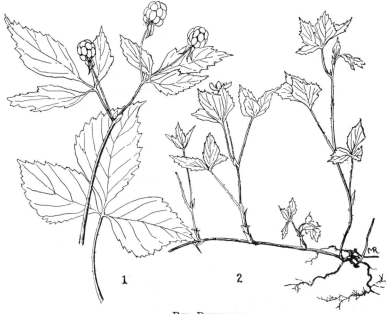

RED DEWBERRY.
1, Leaf and fruit, × ½; 2, Flowering plant, × ¼.

one of our most distinct species, differing in fruit from the
dewberries by the red color.   Although the drupelets adhere
tenaciously to it, the receptacle never becomes edible.

BRISTLY DEWBERRY. *Rubus vermontanus* Blanchard. (*R. nigri-
cans* Gray's New Man.).

These plants of the wet mountain woods and cold swamps
are easily recognized by their ascending habit and very bristly
canes.   The berries are rather inferior to those of the mountain
blackberry.

Rubus setosus Bigelow is similar to the bristly dewberry, but has very glandular pedicels and sepals while the former is usually glandless. This is much less common than the bristly dewberry (*R. vermontanus.*)

BLACK DEWBERRY. Rubus villosus L.

This species occurs in sandy soil in similar locations to the white pine and is more abundant farther south. It is readily recognized by its trailing habit, five thin leaflets, one to four flowers in the cluster, and round, large druped, sweet berries.

SWAMP DEWBERRY. Rubus hispidus L.

This pretty trailing vine of the lowland swamps is easily know by the dark-green, shining, thick leaves with three leaflets which usually remain green throughout the winter. The berries are very small and sour.

THE CULTIVATED BERRIES.

These berries are esteemed more highly for their fruit in this country than in Europe. The European red raspberry has long been cultivated in that country and was early introduced into the United States, but it has been practically driven out by the American cultivated berry, which is more hardy and ripens its fruit in a shorter time. The Cuthbert is one of the leading American red raspberries. The black raspberry is even more important commercially than the red, since it is dried very extensively. The Ohio and the Gregg are standard cultivated forms of the black raspberry. The Shaefer and the Gladstone are supposed to have sprung from the hybrid, *Rubus neglectus.*

The blackberries and dewberries are an American product, the first cultivated blackberry, the Dorchester, being produced in 1841. Some of the best varieties have been evolved from the high-bush blackberry and its allied forms. Here belong the long-cluster blackberries, Taylor and Ancient Briton, the short cluster blackberries, Snyder, Kittatinny, Erie, etc., and the leafy-cluster blackberries, Early Harvest, etc.

Forms of the black dewberry have given us the Lucretia and the Bartel, while the intermediate strain between the high-bush and the black dewberry, usually known as *R. heterophyllus* Willd, has produced the Wilson, Wilson Jr., and Rathburn. While much has been done in improving our native blackberries and raspberries, much more remains to be accomplished, for although the cultivated forms are productive and larger than the wild fruit, still they lack flavor and have much larger seeds.

THE ROSES. ROSA.

Everyone recognizes a rose-bush, even when in the leafless stage, but few—and trained botanists are not always reckoned among these few—can distinguish all of our native species at sight. While this is not always of primary importance, it is worth while with so conspicuous and favorite a flower to know how many kinds may be expected in one's neighborhood, somewhat of their season and natural habitat, whether the particular plant which is under survey is a June rose like the cinnamon or perchance may be of midsummer habit like the swamp rose, whether to be sought by the water side as the swamp rose, or on the dry ridges as the pasture rose, and whether native like the smooth rose or of European ancestry like the sweetbrier. Bearing in mind these characteristics and the others mentioned below we may easily add to the charm of our acquaintance with the wayside rose, the pleasure in most cases of calling it by its own proper name.

1. Flowers single 2
1. Flowers more or less doubled, (introduced species).

Cinnamon rose.

2. Foliage aromatic (sweet-scented) prickles numerous and recurved ....Sweetbrier.
2. Foliage not sweet-scented 3
3. Sepals erected after flowering, persistent; surface of fruit and
   fruit-stalk (pedicel) smooth and stem with few or no
   prickles ....Smooth rose.
3. Sepals spreading after flowering, falling off from the mature
   fruit, surface of fruit and fruit-stalk bristly or hairy, stem
   with prickles 4
4. Stipules narrowly linear, leaflets finely saw-toothed (usually on
   low moist soil) ....Swamp rose.
4. Stipules dilated, leaflets coarsely toothed (usually on dry soil).

Pasture rose.

THE CINNAMON ROSE. *Rosa cinnamomea* L.

Everyone is familiar with this homely old fashioned pink rose. The constancy of its presence about the abandoned homes of the early mountain side clearings is an almost pathetic re-

minder of how our grandmothers must have carried the roots as precious memories from the gardens of their childhood homes when they invaded the wilderness. It is so fully doubled that it seems rarely if ever to spread from seed, but once established the roots send up new shoots year by year, suppressing the un-

CINNAMON ROSE, × ½.

sightly docks and tansy which our herb-drinking ancestors al-always introduced along with it.

THE SWEETBRIER. *Rosa rubiginosa* L.

No plant in all our flora bears a more appropriate name than the sweetbrier, with its combination of strong needle-pointed, hooked prickles, and the spicy fragrance of its foliage. This is evident to the sensitive nostril even when some distance away,

SWEETBRIER.
Flowering branch, × ½.

but when crushed between the fingers is unmistakably suggestive of the fragrance of a highly scented apple. It must have been for this, coupled with its glossy green, that it was brought from Europe into the early New England gardens, for the flowers although pretty are scarcely more attractive than some of our natives. This is sometimes called "Eglantine," although that name more properly belongs to another closely related European species. Being a normal fertile blossom it seeds abundantly, and as a result it has become so frequent in rocky pastures near old homesteads as to be almost a characteristic of them. The mossy galls so often found on the branches are caused by the sting of an insect.

THE SWAMP ROSE. *Rosa carolina* L.

When one comes upon a characteristic colony of this rose in full blossom occupying the front ranks of a water-side thicket, its profusion of pink flowers banked against the dark green of alder and the varnished sprays of the shining willow, or the sheen of the rarer silky willow leaves, it is a picture for long memory. Although either of our other native species may occur in moist soil, this is the one which is characteristically at home along the borders of swamps and streams. This fact, and the further one that the stems are usually tall, often shoulder high, make its general recognition easy.

THE PASTURE ROSE. *Rosa humilis* Marsh.

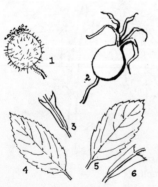

1, PASTURE ROSE, fruit;
2, SMOOTH ROSE, fruit;
3, 4, SWAMP R., stipules and leaflet;
5, 6, PASTURE R., ditto. All × ⅔.

This is the most common wild rose of Vermont pastures and waysides. Its characteristic habitat is dry soil or rocky slopes. The stems are usually low, one to three feet high, slender, armed with straight slender prickles. The pink flowers of this and the other two natives are so similar in size and general appearance that one must turn for careful differentiation to less conspicuous characters. Those of leaf margins and stipules

serve to separate this form from the swamp rose as shown in the
figures and emphasized in the preceding key. The sepals are
most useful for distinguishing this species from the next. In
addition to the characters emphasized in the key one should note
that the outer sepals of the pasture rose are always more or
less lobed.

THE SMOOTH ROSE. *Rosa blanda* Ait.

While less generally common in Vermont than the pasture
rose, the smooth rose is frequent especially on rocky headlands
and banks of lakes and streams. The stems are low, generally one
to three feet, although they may rise somewhat higher than the
pasture rose. The branches typically are nearly or quite unarmed,
but occasional plants occur with numerous prickles. The smooth
surface of the hip and the sepals connivent after the flowering
stage, and persisting even upon the mature fruit, enable ready
recognition as explained in the key. To distinguish this form
from the pasture rose it may suffice to note that the sepals have
entire margins and are not lobed as are the former.

In addition to the above list of the commoner roses several
other native kinds occur occasionally. The most widely distributed of these is the prickly rose, *Rosa acicularis* Lindl. var.
Bourgeauiana Crepin. This is most closely allied to the smooth
rose, differing in the abundance of its long slender prickles and
its bristly leaf stem. This is occasionally found on the dry
headlands and rocky ridges of western Vermont. Two others have
been found so rarely that one who suspects he has them should
refer to some manual of botany, or submit specimens to an authority. The glossy rose, *Rosa virginiana* Mill. has been found
in two places, North Pownal and Stratton Pond. The so-called
"northeastern" or bristly rose, *Rosa nitida* Willd., has been
found only at Bradford.

THE CULTIVATED ROSES.

There are so many kinds of rose in cultivation that only an expert can hope to know them all or to understand their relationships. The sweet brier and the cinnamon rose are so commonly escaped that they are described in detail above. The Gallic or French rose, *Rosa gallica* L. is a low bristly-glandular plant with handsome dark green leaves and fine red flowers, often semi-double, which has occasionally escaped from old gardens to roadsides. The Scotch rose (*Rosa spinosissima* L.) is often cultivated and may become naturalized near houses. The finest of the double roses of garden and greenhouse are either of the damask type (*R. damascena*) or the India or China rose (*R. indica*). The hybrid roses are of these two; the tea roses are of the latter type. The eglantine rose (*R. eglanteria*) is an old fashioned rose with fragrant foliage, resembling the sweet brier. The Japanese rose (*R. rugosa*) is a more recent introduction but rapidly gaining favor because of its rich foliage. Recently the crimson and other ramblers and other clustered roses of the *multiflora* group have been given especial attention. Since they are quite hardy and very attractive and new hybirds are appearing each year, there is much to be hoped for them as additions to the rose garden.

THE THORNAPPLES. CRATAEGUS[1]

This group of plants is best developed in the limestone areas of western Vermont, particularly about Lake Champlain and its tributaries. Occasionally in the Green Mountains they reach an altitude of 2,200 feet, and *Crataegus Kennedyi* Sarg. is known only on the summit of Willoughby Mountain, at about 2,500 feet.

---

[1] Owing to the complexity of the various forms of thornapple, especially in the Champlain valley, it has been necessary either to pass by the group with only a general characterization, or else to make the account more technical than is the balance of this bulletin. The above carefully prepared account of the groups by Mr. Eggleston has been accepted as the best method of treatment under these circumstances.

L. R. J.

Of the ten groups found in Vermont, four are trees and the others are usually large shrubs, although all of them but the Intricatae may occasionally produce a small shrubby tree. This variable genus is not as yet well understood. Although many species have been described, much good work may yet be done in our field to further the study of the thorns. For the purpose of this work it seemed best to give only a short account of the groups. If one cares to go farther he will find in Rhodora, in the Botanical Gazette and in the New Gray's Manual much information which will be pertinent. It should be noted that the following account deals only with the smaller or shrubby species.

Key to the groups of shrubby species based on fruiting characters.

1. Nutlets pitted on the inner surface 2
1. Nutlets plain on the inner surface 3
2. Nutlets deeply pitted ....Macracanthae.
2. Nutlets with shallow pits ....Anomalae.
3. Fruit hard at maturity 4
3. Fruit soft at maturity 5
4. Fruit waxy, petioles smooth ....Pruinosae.
4. Fruit not waxy, petioles wtih stalked glands............Intricatae.
5. Fruit ellipsoidal ....Tenuifoliae
5. Fruit globose ....Rotundifoliae.

Key to the group of shrubby species based on flowering stage.

1. Calyx lobes entire or nearly so 2
1. Calyx lobes serrate 3
2. Leaves yellow-green slightly hairy, flowers 1½—2 cm. wide, anthers, pink ....`..Tenuifoliae.
2. Leaves blue-green, smooth, flowers about 2 cm. wide, anthers light pink ....Pruinosae.
3. Calyx lobes serrate 4
3. Calyx lobes deeply serrate 5
4. Calyx lobes more prominently toothed towards the apex, petioles with stalked glands ....Intricatae.
4. Calyx lobes equally toothed throughout length, petioles without stalked glands ....Rotundifoliae.
5. Leaves dark green and shining above, rather thick, veins somewhat impressed ....Macracanthae.
5. Leaves lighter, thinner, veins not impressed...........Anomalae.

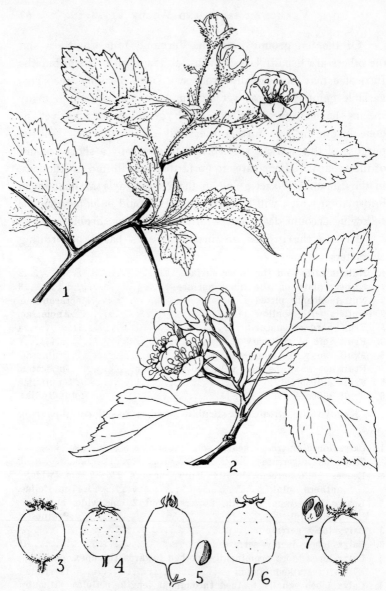

THORNAPPLES. Natural size.
Flowering branches: 1, *Crataegus coccinea*; 2, *Crataegus pruinosa*.
Fruits: 3, *Crataegus coccinea*; 4, *Crataegus rotundifolia*; 5, *Cratae-
gus macrosperma* (fruit and nutlet); 6, *Crataegus pruinosa*; 7,
Crataegus macracantha (fruit and nutlet).

The Intricatae represent a southern group that reaches its northern limit in central Vermont. It has few-flowered corymbs and yellow-green young foliage, both of which are very glandular, stamens usually ten, anthers light yellow. The leaves are elliptical-ovate, acute at both ends, subcoriaceous, the petioles bearing stalked glands. The fruit matures very late, being hard when it falls in October, of a greenish yellow or reddish yellow hue, and globose or short pear-shaped containing three or four nutlets. The shrubs are two to six feet with few thorns. Two species are known in Vermont, *C. apposita* Sarg. and *C. intricata* Lange (*C. coccinea* of the newer edition of Gray's Manual), while one other *C. foetida* Ashe has been reported from the Connecticut valley.

The Rotundifoliae range farther north than any other eastern group and seem well at home in Vermont. The young foliage is yellow-green, corymbs many-flowered, stamens five to twenty, anthers light yellow, leaves elliptical-ovate to orbicular, subcoriaceous, shining above, fruit red, globose, the flesh softening before it falls, ripening from August to October, nutlets three or four. The shrubs are five to fifteen feet high with numerous thorns. *C. Kennedyi* Sarg., *C. Oakesiana* Eggl., *C. irrasa* var *Blanchardi* (Sarg.) Eggl., *C. rotundifolia* Moench., and var *Faxoni* (Sarg.) Eggl., constitute the rotundifoliae of Vermont.

The Tenuifoliae are the most abundant and the most puzzling of our Vermont groups. The young foliage is bronze-green, slightly hairy, the corymbs many flowered, stamens five to twenty, anthers pink, leaves ovate, acute, doubly serrate. The petioles are long and slender. The fruit which matures from August to October, is red, ellipsoidal, calyx erect and slender, flesh soft, the nutlets three to four in number. The shrubs are six to twenty feet high with numerous curved thorns. The following species are known in Vermont: *C. lucorum* var. *insolens* (Sarg.) Eggl., *C. roanensis* Ashe., *C. alnorum* Sarg., *C. macrosperma* Ashe., *C. m.* var. *pentandra* (Sarg.) Eggl., *C. m.* var. *demissa* (Sarg.) Eggl., *C. m.* var. *pastorum* (Sarg.) Eggl., and *C. m.* var. *matura* (Sarg.) Eggl.

The Pruinosae are difficult to distinguish from the Tenuifoliae unless one has the mature fruit. In general the flowers
are larger, the anthers lighter red and the foliage smoother, with
a tendency toward blue-green rather than yellow. The fruit
is waxy, angular or globose, the calyx lobes are raised up and
thickened at the base, and the flesh is hard when the apples fall
in October. The nutlets are usually four or five. The shrubs
are six to twenty feet high with numerous thorns. The species
in Vermont are: *C. pruinosa* (Wendl.) C. Koch., *C. p.* var. *phila-
delphica* (Sarg.) Eggl., *C. p.* var. *dissona* (Sarg.) Eggl., *C.
Beckwithae* Sarg., and *C. Jesupi* Sarg.

The Macracanthae are one of our most distinct groups being
sharply characterized by nutlets with pits on the inner faces,
deeply serrated calyx lobes, and dark green impress-veined,
leathery leaves. The fruit softens in September, is red, globose
and usually contains two or three nutlets, the flesh being quite
characteristic having a glutinous feeling. The plants of this
group more often become trees than the others, being from six
to twenty-five feet in height and with numerous long sharp
thorns. The following species occur in Vermont: *C. macracantha* Loddiges, *C. m.* var. *succulenta* (Schrad) Eggl., and *C. m.*
var. *neofluvialis* (Ashe) Eggl.

The Anomalae are well named as they are our hardest
group to separate. The writer holds that *C. Brainerdi* Sarg. and
its varieties *Egglestoni,* (Sarg.) Rob., *scabrida* (Sarg.) Eggl.,
and *asperifolia* (Sarg.) Eggl. must have originated as crosses between the Macracanthae and perhaps some of the Tenuifoliae;
but they certainly are well established species now, for there are
numerous mountain pastures in Vermont where hundreds of
the variety *Egglestoni* are found, and the others are nearly as
frequent and as well marked in various localities. The Anomalae
have thinner, less shiny leaves and calyx lobes less cut than the
Macracanthae, while the pits of the nutlets are shallow and the
flesh is not glutinous.

RUE FAMILY. RUTACEAE

This is an interesting family of plants, chiefly trees and shrubs, including the citrus fruits, orange and lemon, the fraxinella of old-fashioned gardens and the garden rue from which comes the family name. This rue was probably more commonly cultivated formerly than now and it has established itself in at least one place (Weybridge) as a garden escape. The leaves or other parts are characterized by transparent dots which contain a pungent aromatic oil. Only one representative occurs in Vermont.

THE PRICKLY-ASH. *Xanthoxylum americanum* Mill.   . .

This is a shrub of three to eight feet usually forming thickets on rocky woods and banks. It is frequent in portions of the Champlain valley. This is readily recognized by its prickly stem and strongly aromatic bark and leaves, the latter being compound, somewhat like the ash only smaller, hence the name. The American Indians used the prickly ash as a medicine and it became one of the popular home remedies of the herb-doctors of the early settlements, an infusion of the bark being used for ulcerous wounds, rheumatism, colic, etc. The bark was sometimes chewed as a remedy for toothache, and it is therefore

PRICKLY ASH.
Fruiting twig, × ½.

sometimes known as the toothache-tree. One who has recently tried it says that it excites the flow of saliva and drives away the toothache, at least temporarily, but that the taste of the bark is scarcely less disagreeable than the ache it relieves.

CROWBERRY FAMILY. EMPETRACEAE

BLACK CROWBERRY.   HEATH-BERRY.   *Empetrum nigrum* L.

This is a prostrate, heath-like, evergreen, alpine shrub with black berries found in the moist, peaty soil on the summits of Mount Mansfield and Camel's Hump. The evergreen leaves are very small, less than one-fourth of an inch in diameter. The fruit is said to be a favorite food of the mountain birds.

SUMACH FAMILY. ANACARDIACEAE

This is an interesting family of plants, mainly tropical. Several species have a resinous juice which thickens upon exposure and furnishes the finest of oriental varnishes, including those most prized from Japan and China.   All of these are, however, related to our own poison ivy and, like that, may be poisonous to the skin of certain persons. The cashew and pistachio nuts and the mango fruit are also valuable products from oriental members of this family.   As it occurs in Vermont it is represented by but one genus.

THE SUMACHS. RHUS.

These are among our most familiar shrubs. The several species may be distinguished as follows:

1. Flowers and fruit in compact clusters at the end of branches, fruit reddish and hairy, plants not poisonous to the touch, (the true sumachs) 2
1. Flowers and fruit in loose clusters in the leaf axils, fruit whitish and smooth, plants poisonous, (the poison sumachs)........5
2. Leaves compounded of three leaflets...........Fragrant sumach.
2. Leaves compounded of seven or more leaflets 3
3. Petioles winged or margined ....Dwarf sumach.
3. Petioles not winged or margined 4
4. Branches and leaf-stalks velvety-hairy...........Staghorn sumach.
4. Branches and leaf-stalks smooth ....Smooth sumach.
5. Leaves compounded of three leaflets ....,......Poison ivy.
5. Leaves compounded of 7 to 13 leaflets ....Poison sumach.

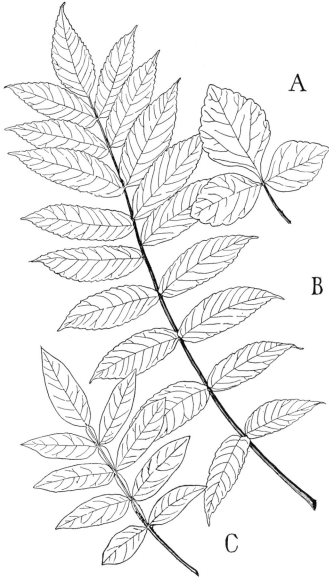

A, FRAGRANT SUMACH;   B, SMOOTH SUMACH;
C, DWARF SUMACH, × ½.

STAGHORN SUMACH. *Rhus typhina* L.

This is the common sumach of Vermont, forming thickets everywhere by waysides and in old fields. While usually developing as a shrub of ten feet or less when in thickets, it may

STAGHORN SUMACH.
Fruiting branch, × ⅓.

assume the habit and size of a small tree when standing alone. The farmer must often rate the sumach as a nuisance because of its invasion of his pastures and the persistence with which, following cutting, it will sprout from the root. The lover of the wayside, however, must prize the grace and beautiful tints of the sumach foliage and the richer color of its fruits in autumn and winter. The sumachs are indeed among the best of native shrubs for ornamental planting. In selecting plants the fertile or fruit-bearing ones should usually be chosen. A finely cut-leaved form is obtainable from nurserymen. The leaves and the bark, which are rich in tannin, were formerly used in tanning, and a medicine for fever has been prepared from the root.

SMOOTH SUMACH. *Rhus glabra* L.

This is quite as handsome a shrub as the staghorn and is preferable for ornamental planting. It does not grow quite so large and has a more spreading irregular habit. It occurs only rarely in northern Vermont but is common in the Hoosac and Southern Connecticut valleys. A cut-leaved form of this species is also found in the trade. The leaves were formerly used for tanning and the berries, because of their acidity, were employed as a substitute for lemon juice in various domestic practices and in the preparation of home remedies. The berries are used in dyeing, an infusion being said to furnish an unequalled black dye for wool.

DWARF SUMACH. *Rhus copallina* L.

This as its name implies is a lower shrub than either of the above mentioned. It is frequent in Vermont in dry or sandy soil and is easily recognized by the winged margins of the leaf stalks. Its value for ornamental planting is on a par with the staghorn or smooth species. Its leaves are quite as rich in tannin, and large quantities are collected in the south for tanning leather. The Indians were fond of admixing dwarf or smooth sumach leaves with their smoking tobacco.

FRAGRANT SUMACH. *Rhus canadensis* Marsh. (*R aromatica* Ait.)

This is a low straggling shrub, usually two to four feet high, which occurs only occasionally on rocky banks in western Vermont. It is of considerable value in ornamental planting in rocky soil, but otherwise is of less economic interest than the other sumachs. Its popular name was suggested by the fact that the leaves, especially when bruised, are slightly aromatic.

POISON IVY. *Rhus toxicodendron* L.

The poison ivy, or three-leaved ivy, is sometimes given the confusing name of poison oak. It is common, especially in moist woodlands and fence rows, and is so dangerous a plant that every school child should learn to recognize it. This is easily done by noting the characters of leaf and fruit. The leaflets are always in threes, with the end leaflet slightly stalked, as shown in the figure. In size and toothing they have a general resemblance to the common woodbine or five-leaved ivy. The number of leaflets is, however, a sure distinction. The poison ivy is distinguishable from other three-leaved woodland plants by its woody stem and climbing habit. Its dry, greenish-white berries, the size of small peas, standing in grape-like clusters, are also a conspicuous character of the older plants. In the matter of climbing, however, the plant may vary so widely as to puzzle botanists. It may stand as a low upright shrub if it has nothing to cling to, but usually it develops as a low vine, climbing by rooting stems over old stumps and walls. If well started at the base of a living tree it may, however, climb to indefinite height, rooting itself in the bark and injuring the tree as well as menacing human passers-by. Some persons are severely poisoned by the slightest contact with this shrub, while others handle it with impunity. Even the latter may well shun it, however, since if once poisoned they will thereafter remain susceptible. The poison resides in a resinous exudate on the sur-

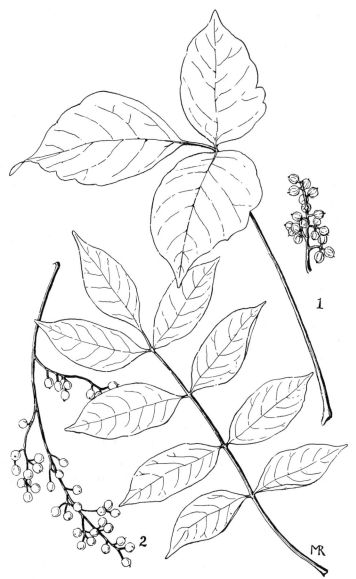

1, POISON IVY;   2, POISON SUMACH.

Leaf and fruit of each, $\times$ ½.

face of the plant, and, according to our best authorities, it is transmitted only by contact, i. e. not blown through the air. In many cases especially susceptible persons are probably unwittingly poisoned by getting it on their shoes or clothing and, later, poisoning their hands by contact with these. Most persons are especially liable to the poison when perspiring freely. After wandering in proximity to the plant at such a time, it is a wise precaution thoroughly to wash hands and face with free use of strong soap or, much better, with washing soda or some other strongly alkaline solution, which will remove the poison before it has time to strike in. If too late for this, the best remedy is to bathe the parts freely with some of these alkaline washes. A solution of sugar of lead in alcohol is one of the best. Where the poison-ivy occurs near schools or dwellings, it should be exterminated. If in the open field this is easily done by digging it out. Often, however, it grows in stone walls among stunps, or so close to the base of a tree that it is difficult to get at the roots. In such cases a liberal application of a strong solution of washing soda will destroy it. A solution of arseniate of soda (1 pound in 8 gallons of water) is even more effective.

THE POISON SUMACH. *Rhus Vernix* L.

This also goes under a confusing variety of names, such as poison elder and poison dogwood. It likewise exudes a poison similar to the preceding and is fully as dangerous. This shrub grows to a height of six to fifteen feet. It is a swamp plant familiar to anyone who penetrates the swampy thickets bordering Lake Champlain. Fortunately it is not common in most parts of Vermont. It is the most graceful of the family, with brilliant autumn tints. Were it not so poisonous it would be highly prized as an ornamental shrub. The white berries resemble those of the commoner poison ivy but are borne in longer, looser clusters.

HOLLY FAMILY. ILICINAE

Many persons who are familiar with the name and appearance of the holly tree of Europe and the South do not know that there are two shrubs of this family in Vermont, the winterberry and the mountain holly. Although neither rivals the hollies just referred to for Christmas decorations, each is an attractive plant in its way and season.

WINTERBERRY. *Ilex verticillata* (L.) Gray.

This is also called the black alder, but should not be confused with the true alder (*Alnus*), or with the elder berries (*Sambucus*). It is a frequent shrub in moist thickets, of an upright habit, much branched, four to eight feet high, with grayish

bark and dark green leaves, conspicuously veined and somewhat leathery. The southern holly is evergreen, but the leaves fall from our northern species in autumn. The berries, which ripen in September to a bright scarlet, are about one-fourth inch in diameter. They may form singly or in close clusters of two or

WINTERBERRY.
Fruiting branch, × ½.

three in the axils of the leaves, where they cling through the autumn and even in the winter may render the shrubs conspicuous and of ornamental value. Both the bark and berries have a decidedly bitter taste and were formerly used in home medicines for fevers. This species is somewhat variable, with one named variety in Vermont (var. *tenuifolia*).

MOUNTAIN HOLLY. *Nemopanthus mucronata* (L.) Trelease
(*N. fascicularis* Raf.)

This is a frequent shrub in cool moist woods and swamps, somewhat taller than the last. It bears abundant crops of ber-

ries which are about one-fourth inch in diameter, ripening in mid-August to a beautiful
dark crimson and making the bushes very
showy. They are easily distinguished from the allied winter-berry by the fact that each berry
is borne on a stalk an inch or more long, which
is crimson like the fruit. The berries though
not poisonous are more or less bitter and repugnant. It deserves a place in ornamental
MOUNTAIN   planting.
HOLLY, × ⅔.

STAFF TREE FAMILY. CELASTRACEAE

CLIMBING BITTERSWEET.   STAFF-VINE.   *Celastrus scandens* L.

This is the only representative in Vermont of its family. It
is the most elegant of the native vines, frequently found climbing over rocks and bushes and even ascending small trees to
fifteen or twenty feet. Often it twines about other stems so

closely as to deform them in
curious ways. It prefers moist
shady situations but it will
grow almost anywhere. The
leaf characters are shown in
the drawing. The fruits are
bright orange, nearly one-half
inch in diameter and when
mature in late autumn the
outer part bursts to disclose
the still brighter scarlet berry-
like contents. These are
in small cluster which, persisting into the winter, give a
unique charm to this vine for

CLIMBING BITTERSWEET.
Fruiting branch, × ½.

ornamental planting as a cover for rockeries, arbors and piazzas.
They may be cut in autumn and brought into the house for dry

bouquets. The berries are non-poisonous but distasteful. Formerly they were used in compounding home remedies which were destined to "cleanse the blood" and act upon a torpid liver.

MAPLE FAMILY. SAPINDACEAE

The most familiar members of this family are trees and were described in the bulletin, "Trees of Vermont." Two of the maples, striped maple or whistle-wood and mountain maple,

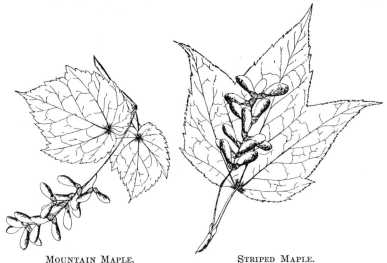

MOUNTAIN MAPLE.   STRIPED MAPLE.
Leaves and fruit, × ⅓.   Leaf and fruit, × ⅓.

never grow large and are often shrubby in habit. Leaf cuts of these are therefore reproduced from the previous bulletin. There is another interesting member of this family which is always a shrub, i. e. the bladdernut.

BLADDER-NUT. *Staphylea trifolia* L.

This shrub differs widely from the tree maples and, indeed, was formerly classed with the bittersweet in the preceding family. It is a handsome, upright, branching shrub of six to fifteen feet, found occasionally in moist woods and thickets. Its leaves are compounded of three leaflets somewhat resembling poison ivy.

The character which will make its recognition sure, however, is the fruit. This is a triangular capsule one to two inches long, consisting of three papery-walled pods grown together. Usually the seeds in two of these pods are abortive, while that in the third

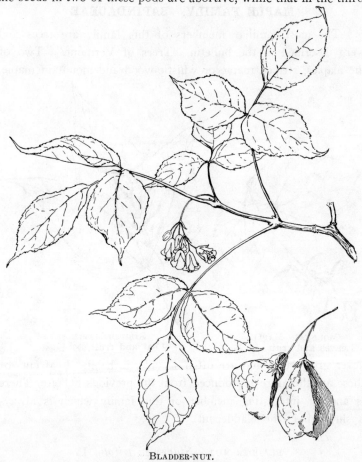

BLADDER-NUT.
Flowering branch and fruit, × ½.

is the size of a small pea. This may loosen as it ripens converting the pod into a curious natural rattlebox. The adaptation of this peculiarity of structure to the dissemination of the seed, whether through the agency of air or water, is evident.

BUCKTHORN FAMILY. RHAMNACEAE

The buckthorn proper is a European tree or large shrub which is frequently planted and has sometimes escaped to Vermont waysides and so was described in "Trees of Vermont." A native buckthorn and two related shrubs further represent the family in our territory.

ALDER-LEAVED BUCKTHORN.
Rhamnus alnifolia L'Her.

The native buckthorn occurs rather frequently in cold swamps. It is a low shrub, reaching four or five feet in height and tending to grow in clumps. The leaf-form as shown in the sketch resembles that of the alder, whence its name. The flowers appear with the leaves in early spring, but are small and greenish, therefore scarcely noticeable. The fruit consists of berries about the size of peas, borne in

ALDER-LEAVED BUCKTHORN, × ½.

clusters each on a stem about one-half inch long. These mature in midsummer when they become black and pulpy, more tempting in appearance than in flavor. No use has been made of this plant, although its European relatives yield both medicines and dyes.

CEANOTHUS

There are two species of *Ceanothus* in Vermont each of some interest, distinguishable as follows:

Branches and underside of leaves more or less downy, flowering in
    July, a common shrub of dry woodlands....New Jersey tea.
Branches and leaves smooth or nearly so, flowering in May, a rare
    shrub of the sandy bluffs of Lake Champlain.Smaller red root.

NEW JERSEY TEA. *Ceanothus americanus* L.

This is a common under-shrub in dry open woodlands, especially in somewhat sandy soil. The characters of its leaf and of the dry three-sided fruit are shown in the illustration. The

small and white flowers hang in clusters at the end of a rather long stalk. Each flower in turn stands upon a white, thread-like stem. The leaves of this plant were used as a substitute for tea during the Revolution; hence its common name. It is also known as red-root because of the deep red color of the bark of the roots, which is said to be used in Canada to dye wool. It has mildly astringent qualities and has been used as a medicine.

NEW JERSEY TEA.
In fruit, × ½.

SMALLER RED-ROOT. *Ceanothus ovatus* Desf.

This is a similar shrub to the preceding, but of lower growth, smooth throughout and bearing shorter flower stalks. It is a rare shrub, confined to a small area of the sandy bluffs of Lake Champlain in Burlington Bay. It is of peculiar botanical interest since it is a plant typical rather of the western prairies and the shores of the Great Lakes, and because its presence on Champlain shores possibly dates from the time when this lake was an arm of the northern ocean and in closer relation with what is now the western lake region.

VINE FAMILY. VITACEAE

Th general likeness of our two representatives of this family, the grapes and Virginia creepers, would lead any close observer to class them together. They are vines climbing by compound tendrils which are borne opposite the leaves—a family mark—and all bear fruit of similar structure and appearance. The well marked difference is that the grapes have simple leaves while the Virginia creeper leaves are compounded of five leaflets.

THE GRAPES.

The grapes reach their best development in a warmer climate than this, yet in right locations in Vermont both the wild and certain cultivated varieties of grape flourish. When one recalls that the splendid European raisin and wine grapes, now so much grown in California with berries as large as small plums, originated from an Asiatic species having berries not larger than currants, and that all the grapes cultivated in eastern America have been produced within a century from wild American species, he may readily believe that in time hardier and better varieties, which will thrive and ripen anywhere in our territory, will be secured from American stock.

The three native wild species may be distinguished as follows:

1. Leaves densely rusty-woolly on under side............Fox grape.
1. Leaves not rusty woolly ....2.
2. Leaves pale or glaucous on under side..........Summer grape.
2. Leaves green on under side ....River grape.

RIVER GRAPE. *Vitis vulpina* L. (*V. riparia* Mx.)

This is the commonest wild grape of Vermont. It passes under several common names; riverbank grape, from its favorite habitat; frost grape, from its late ripening which may come after the early frosts; sweet-scented grape, from the delightful fragrance of the flowers which open with the June roses. It will grow in a wide variety of soils and situations but is most

at home along the banks of streams and in alluvial thickets. Here
it climbs to any height necessary to reach the sunlight and bears
abundant crops of small berries, about one-third of an inch in
diameter.   These vary widely in flavor from sour to fairly

RIVER GRAPE, × ⅖.

sweet, but are generally austere.   The river grape is distinguishable from the summer grape both by leaf characters and by the
later fruit which ripens with the autumn frosts. The foliage
has a bright green cast, the leaves having a thin, broadly heart-
shape depression at the base, more or less three-lobed or five-lobed,
with sharply cut notches, smooth and bright green below except
that the veins and their angles may be hairy. The leaf margins
are variously toothed and cut, the teeth and the long terminal
point of the leaf being sharply acute.   The fruits are often
gathered for preserves or for the juice. The Clinton and some
other cultivated grapes are derived from this stock.

SUMMER GRAPE. *Vitis bicolor* Le Conte.

The summer grape is frequent, especially in dry, gravelly soil and about the bases of cliffs. The berries ripen just before the frosts. They are small, one-half inch or less in diameter, with a dense bloom and of sour but pleasant flavor when ripe. The

young canes usually, but not always, have a bluish or glaucous bloom. The leaves are rougher than the last owing to the deeper veining, and are a darker green above and lighter glaucous-blue below. The bluish bloom may, however, disappear from cane and leaf in the autumn. The leaves may be quite smooth or with scattering rusty hairs on the underside. The tendrils and

SUMMER GRAPE, × ½.

leaf stalks are relatively long. The leaves on the younger growth are often deeply three-to-five-lobed with the base of the clefts rounded, those on the older growths shallowly three-lobed. The margins are almost entire, or have shallow and relatively dull teeth as compared with the river grape.

FOX GRAPE. *Vitis labrusca* L.

This is a grape found commonly from Massachusetts south and westward. It has been reported in Vermont only from Vernon. The leaves and young shoots of this grape are very cottony, and even the adult leaves retain the rusty wool beneath. The fruit is large usually with a tough musky pulp, but varying widely. From it by breeding and selection have come most of the cultivated American grapes, as for example the Concord.

THE VIRGINIA CREEPERS. AMERICAN IVY. PSEDERA. (AMPELOPSIS).

The Virginia creeper is the predominant vine of Vermont, everywhere clothing uncouth walls and fences with its green mantle and festooning decaying buildings and decrepit trees with its fresh sprays. It is sometimes known as woodbine, American ivy or five-leaved ivy. A glance at the illustration will serve

VIRGINIA CREEPER.
Leaf and fruit of the smooth disk-creeper, × ½.

to show its characters to anyone in doubt as to its identity. Its autumn colors add much to its charm, making it by all means the most useful vine for general ornamental planting in Vermont. It has long been observed that there are some differences between vines especially as to the clinging habits, and recently two species which occur in Vermont have been recognized and named.

Since popular names have not been applied to these we have coined them as follows:

1. Tendril branches twining, disks few or none....Tendril creeper.
2. Tendril branches mostly ending in adhesive disks.
                                                        Disk-creeper.

TENDRIL CREEPER. *Psedera vitacea* (Kneer) Greene.

This is the commonest form in Vermont, especially in wayside thickets and old fence rows. While usually clambering over low fences and thickets it may ascend tall trees, clinging to any available small support by the three to five slender twining branchlets of the non-disk-bearing tendrils. This is the creeper most commonly transplanted but either of the two disk forms is to be preferred for many situations. The tendril creeper has slightly larger leaves and fruit than the disk forms.

DISK-CREEPER. *Psedera quinquefolia* (L.) Greene.

When a vine is desired to climb the side of a house, wall, tree or similar surface, the disk-bearing varieties should be sought. The type or smooth one is frequent, ascending tree trunks in open woodlands. There is also a downy variety (var. *hirsuta*) which occurs especially about cliffs, where it may be seen ascending vertical walls of bare rock with no support other than its own disks. It often develops aerial rootlets which further aid it in climbing. Apparently it is not so common as either of the others and is said not to produce berries. Further observations are needed upon this and other matters concerning the distribution and characters of these creepers.

ROCK-ROSE FAMILY. CISTACEAE

BEACH-HEATHER. *Hudsonia tomentosa* Nutt.

This plant is also known as the downy hudsonia. As its English name implies, this is a heather-like plant which is found only along the sandy beaches of Lake Champlain. So far as observed it is confined to the vicinity of Burlington bay and the sandy stretches just northward in the neighborhood of the mouth of the Winooski river. There it forms curious mound-shaped colonies, sometimes several feet across, which enlarge and elevate themselves year by year by dint of capturing the drifting sand in their meshwork of fine branches. The leaves are very small, scale-like, and grayish from the downy hairs, characters which are doubtless helpful in protecting them from sun and drought. In early summer an abundance of tiny yellow blossoms transform each tuft into a mound of gold. This plant, like the smaller red-root, is an interesting evidence of the relation of the Champlain flora to that of the sea shore and the Great Lakes, since it occurs nowhere else between these points.

MEZEREUM FAMILY. THYMELAEACEAE

This is a rather curious group of plants distinguished by a bark of great toughness and acridity. Two representatives are to be included for Vermont.

LEATHERWOOD. *Dirca palustris* L.

This is often called moosewood in Vermont. It is a low, much branched shrub of three to five feet in height, frequent in low moist woodlands. The pale greenish-yellow flowers, about one-half inch long, appear in early spring making the bush temporarily conspicuous, but they rapidly fade and fall as the leaves appear. The leaves are smooth and handsome, green above, pale and slightly downy beneath. The bark is the most remarkable development of its kind among our native plants. It is very thick and consists of long interlaced fibres of surprising strength. So tough is it

LEATHER WOOD, × ½ that the united strength of two men will scarcely break the bark removed from a well developed stem. It was used for thongs, ropes and basketry by the aborigines, and supplied bag strings for the millers and farmers of the early settlements. The plant was used by the Indians for its medicinal qualities, being chewed for toothache and possessing emetic properties.

Closely allied to this leatherwood is the

DAPHNE OR LADY LAUREL. *Daphne Mezereum* L.

This is a small, erect, garden shrub, with attractive lilac-purple flowers clinging closely to the twigs in earliest spring and, later, bearing clean handsome foliage. It has escaped from old gardens to rocky woodlands in a few places in the state (Burlington and Montpelier). Probably the seed is carried by birds feeding on the berries.

OLEASTER FAMILY. ELAEAGNACEAE

CANADIAN BUFFALO-BERRY. *Shepherdia canadensis* (L.) Nutt.

This family is closely allied to the preceding and like it has but the one native species in Vermont. This is a comparatively rare plant on the cliffs and headlands of the Champlain valley. It is characterized by the rusty appearance of the lower leaf surface, due to the abundant clothing of silver stellate hairs which are interesting as viewed under the microscope. The fruit, which is borne but sparingly, is a yellowish red, insipid berry. This plant is sometimes recommended for ornamental planting on dry rocky situations. It is, however, less used than is its close relative, the buffalo-berry of the western plains, which is valuable both for its silvery foliage and its edible fruit.

LOOSESTRIFE FAMILY. LYTHRACEAE

SWAMP LOOSESTRIFE. *Decodon verticillatus* (L) Ellg.

The members of this family are typically herbaceous, but one of the most attractive, the swamp loosestrife or water willow. *Decodon verticillatus* (L.) Ellg., is woody at the base and has the general appearance of a small shrub. It has lithe branches and long slender leaves, giving it a willow-like aspect. It chooses a similar habitat in the borders of swamps, or with its roots buried in a sphagnum bog. A glance at its opposite leaves serves, however, to differentiate it from the alternate-leaved willow twig, and its beautiful magenta blossoms add a glory to many a swamp in August. These have an added interest because of their three forms, which show remarkable adaptation to cross fertilization by insects. It is one of the most attractive plants for ornamental planting along streams or similar wet places.

DOGWOOD FAMILY. CORNACEAE

The name dogwood is misapplied to other shrubs in Vermont[1], which is the more unfortunate since there are seven native species of true dogwoods, including some of our commonest and handsomest shrubs. These are all characterized by having white or greenish-white four-parted flowers, which are individually rather small but are collected in conspicuous clusters. The fruit follows also in showy clusters of berries, the color and size varying with the species. The dogwoods bear a general resemblance to the arrowwoods or viburnums, described later in this pamphlet, from which the fruit will most readily serve to distinguish them. The stone of the viburnum berries is much flattened, one-celled and one-seeded; that of the dogwoods is oval, two-celled and two-seeded. It is also helpful to remember that all the dogwoods have entire leaf margins.

The several native species of dogwood are recognizable as follows:

---

[1] The striped maple is often called striped dogwood; the poison sumach is also known as poison dogwood.

1. Flowers in a close head, appearing like a single large blossom 1 to 3 inches across, with small greenish flowers in the center surrounded by four large petal-like white leaves (involucre); fruit bright red ....2.
1. Flowers white in a broad, flat, open, cluster; fruit white or blue ....3.
2. A large shrub or small tree of 10 to 30 feet.
Flowering dogwood.
2. Small, less than 1 foot high........................Bunch-berry.
3. Leaves alternate........ ....Alternate-leaved dogwood.
3. Leaves opposite ....4.
4. Leaves broadly ovate (egg-shaped) often nearly round; fruit light blue ....Round-leaved dogwood.
4. Leaves narrower; fruit pale blue or blue-white ....5.
5. Twigs, leaf stalks and lower leaf-surfaces silky-downy, often rusty; fruit pale blue ....Silky dogwood.
5. Twigs smooth and leaves smooth or nearly so; fruit white or lead-color ....6.
6. Branches red or purplish, leaves rounded at base.
Red-osier dogwood.
6. Branches gray, leaves tapering at base........Panicled dogwood.

FLOWERING DOGWOOD. *Cornus florida* L.

This is the most showy of the dogwoods and is known and famed for its beauty wherever it occurs. It is common from Massachusetts southward, but in Vermont it occurs only sparingly in the southeastern and southwestern counties. It will, however, grow if introduced farther north and deserves to be so planted much more commonly than has yet been done. It is a clean, shapely bush or small tree, and the profusion of its snowy white flower clusters in late spring and of scarlet fruit in the fall makes it a conspicuous and charming feature of the landscape. So safe a harbinger of spring is it, that the Indians taught the early settlers to plant their corn when the dogwood blossomed. Many interesting uses have been made of the flowering dogwood other than for ornament. Its bark supplies an excellent tonic, said almost to rival quinine. Indeed the early botanical explorer, Peter Kalm, says that the colonists had such faith in the virtues of dogwood that "when the cause fell down in spring for want of strength the people tie a branch of this tree to their necks thinking it will help them." When powdered it has been used as a dentifrice, and a bunch of the smaller twigs has been found by the Virginian negroes an efficient tooth brush. The bark steeped with iron sulphate makes a good black ink, and from the bark of the smaller roots a scarlet dye was made by the Indians. The wood is very hard, of fine texture and prized for turning and for tool handles.

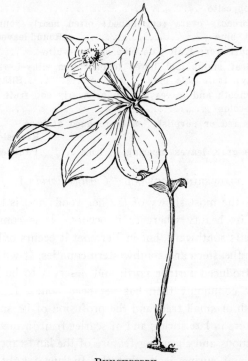

BUNCHBERRY.
Flowering plant, × ½.

BUNCHBERRY. *Cornus canadensis* L.

This is often also called the dwarf cornel since it is the only one of so dwarf a size. Indeed it scarcely seems proper to call this a woody plant at all, inasmuch as only the slender creeping stem below ground is woody.   It is a familiar plant in cool, moist woodlands from the lowest altitudes to the mountain summits. Its charm begins with the opening of the flower clusters in May, or on the higher mountain slopes in June, and increases with the maturing of the compact bunches of scarlet fruit.   The bright berries are a favorite with children, by whom they are sometimes eaten, being palatable with a slightly sweetish taste though rather insipid and seedy.   They are also sometimes made into puddings.

ALTERNATE-LEAVED DOGWOOD.
Fruiting branch, × ½.

ALTERNATE-LEAVED DOGWOOD.   *Cornus alternifolia L.f.*

This is frequent in moist, wayside thickets and open woodlands.   It forms a beautiful shrub of five to fifteen feet, or even a small tree when in the open, the lateral branches tending to form successive horizontal stages. The broad, flat clusters of small,

white flowers, followed by the blue-black fruit about one-third
of an inch in diameter, serve to show that it is a dogwood. The
leaf arrangement differs from those of any other species in
that the leaves are alternate, forming close clusters near the end
of the branch. The form and size of the leaves is shown in the
figure. They are nearly smooth above and whitish and minutely
hairy below. The branches are usually greenish streaked with
white. The beautiful browns of the young shoots and the similar
tints returning in autumn add to the charms which combine to
make it one of the most attractive of the native shrubs for ornamental planting.

ROUND-LEAVED DOGWOOD.   *Cornus circinata* L'Her.

This is a shrub of four to eight feet, common along waysides
and in woodlands.   The small white flowers are borne in rather

ROUND-LEAVED DOGWOOD.
Leaf and fruit, × ½.

dense flat clusters, two to three inches across. The fruit is a
pale blue, or it may turn to a whitish color, many of the berries

being abortive. The branches are greenish, profusely blotched with purple and usually warty-dotted. The leaves are opposite, broadly ovate and often nearly round, or sometimes even wider than long, abruptly pointed, slightly downy above and pale and densely soft-woolly below. It is a clean attractive shrub whether ornamenting wayside thickets or for landscape planting. The bark, like that of the preceding species, has sometimes been used in medicine as a tonic.

SILKY DOGWOOD. *Cornus amomum* Miller (*C. sericea* L.)

This is also known as swamp dogwood in recognition of its preference for a moist habitat, bordering damp woods and keeping the button bush company along the streams. It occurs also on higher ground. It is a branching shrub with stems somewhat purplish, rising three to ten feet. Its name comes from the silky down which typically clothes the young twigs and lower leaf surfaces. The berries, when mature, are about one-fourth inch in diameter and of a pale blue hue. The bark has sometimes been used in medicine as a tonic in the same way as has that of the two preceding species. The Indians so employed it. They also made a black dye from the bark and a scarlet one from the rootlets. Kinnikinnik is the aboriginal name for a favorite smoking mixture of the Indians, consisting of tobacco and the scrapings of the wood of the silky dogwood, a name which has been given a permanent place in geography as the name of a Wisconsin town.

RED-OSIER DOGWOOD. *Cornus stolonifera* Michx.

The red-osier dogwood is a spreading shrub from four to eight feet high, usually with the lower parts of the stem prostrate and soon rooting to form clumps of indefinite expanse. This creeping habit of the stems gave it its Latin name. The slender osier-like appearance and the characteristic reddish color gave rise to the English name. The flower clusters are white, usually relatively small; the berries, one-fourth inch in diameter, ripening to white or lead color. A taste thereof will prove their unpalatability, yet it is said that the western Indians rated them among their foods. A French chemist has shown that the fruit

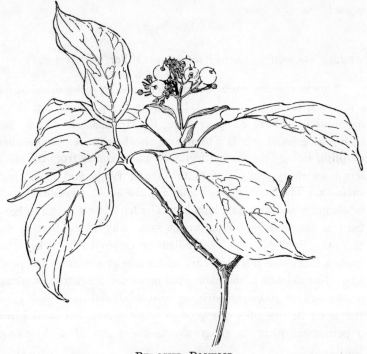

RED-OSIER DOGWOOD.
Fruiting branch, × ½.

yields one-third its weight of an oil similar to olive oil. The chief interest attaching to this plant, however, is because of the increasing use made of it for ornamental purposes. Both in nature and for landscape planting it is highly attractive whether in summer or winter and its spreading habit adds much to its value for certain situations.

PANICLED DOGWOOD. *Cornus paniculata* L'Her.

This is a slender, much-branched, erect plant, four to eight feet high, commonly bordering highways and riverbank thickets.

The smooth gray branches, rather narrow leaves whitish beneath, numerous close clusters of white flowers and white fruit borne on a pale scarlet stalk, serve to make it comparatively easy of distinction. It adds an attractive feature to the natural landscape and is excellent for ornamental planting, but no other use has been made of it.

PANICLED DOGWOOD.
Branch with fruit, × ½.

HEATH FAMILY. ERICACEAE

This includes the largest group of Vermont shrubs except the rose family. Like that it has many valuable species, whether for fruit or ornament, and some quite puzzling to one who attempts to know all the shrubs at sight. To facilitate the solution of such puzzles the following key to the shrubby genera has been prepared and under each genus there is, in addition, a key to the species.

Some of the other heaths not here included are slightly woody, notably the prince's pine (*Chimaphila*) which is a pretty evergreen, about six inches high, common in sandy woodlands, and the shin leaves (*Pyrola*). There are several species of the latter closely resembling each other in general characters. Some of them have leaves so similar to the arbutus as to confuse the mayflower hunter, while others look more like the wintergreen. Very similar to the heath and closely related thereunto is the little diapensia, whose dainty dark green cushions dotted with large white blossoms is reward enough for any flower lover who may venture to visit the alpine peak of Mt. Mansfield during the last of May.

KEY TO THE GENERA OF SHRUBBY HEATHS.

1. Fruit a berry or berry-like ....2.
1. Fruit a dry capsule ....5.
2. Calyx below the ovary, leaves evergreen ....Bearberry
2. Calyx borne upon or inclosing the ovary and appearing as teeth crowning the edible berry ....3.
3. Berries white; leaves evergreen ....Snowberry.
3. Berries blue or black; leaves deciduous.
         Blueberries and huckleberries.
3. Berries red; leaves evergreen ....4.
4. Berries tart, 4-celled, crowned by 4 small calyx teeth, leaves less than ½ inch long ....Cranberries
4. Berries spicy-aromatic, 5-celled and surrounded by 5 conspicuous calyx lobes, leaves 1 inch or more in length....Wintergreen.
5. Flowers small, less than ¼ inch wide, petals united into an urn-shaped or cylindrical tube with contracted mouth..........6.
5. Flower larger, ⅜ to 2 inches wide, open and spreading above....8.
6. Flowers ½ inch in diameter nearly globular........Male berry.
6. Flowers larger and more elongated ....7.
7. Leaves white beneath with margins rolled back....Wild rosemary.
7. Leaves scurfy both sides, not white beneath, flat....Leather leaf.
8. Flowers without tube and much broader than long (saucer or wheel-shaped) ....9.
8. Flowers tubular or contracted below, spreading above, (salver, funnel or bell-shaped) ....10.
9. Petals nearly or quite distinct, leaves coated underneath with woolly hairs ....Labrador tea.
9. Petals united, leaves smooth ....Laurels.
10. Small trailing plant ....Trailing arbutus.
10. Erect shrubs ....The rhododendrons.

BEARBERRY. *Arctostaphylos uva-ursi* (L.) Spreng.

The bearberry is a trailing plant forming close mats on dry, barren or rocky soil. The woody stems, one to two feet long, are slender but rise from a strong central root. The leaves are small, thick, smooth, shining and evergreen. The flowers are small, drooping and white or rose color. The fruit ripens in late summer to a red color and is about the size of a pea. It is abundant and, since it persists through the winter with the glossy evergreen leaves, it is a conspicuous and well-marked shrub. The bearberry is common in the north of Europe, and the leaves have there been used from ancient times as a diuretic and astringent tonic. Their abundant tannin content has caused them to be collected in large quantities

RED BEARBERRY, × ⅔.

in Russia, Scandinavia and Iceland for use in tanning the finer leathers. They are also used for brown and black dyes. The North American Indians mixed the leaves with their smoking tobacco, as they did the silky dogwood, under the name of Kinnikinnik. The berries are dry, mealy and insipid, but are eaten by partridges and other birds in winter. The bearberry is a handsome ornamental shrub for planting in dry rocky situations.

WINTERGREEN. *Gaultheria procumbens* L.

The creeping wintergreen is a common plant in cool damp woods, especially in sandy soil. It is familiar to every child where it occurs, and is so easily distinguished by the characteristic spicy, aromatic "wintergreen flavor" of berries and leaves, especially the younger ones, that no description is necessary to insure its recognition. It goes under various other common names, of which checkerberry is the one most used in Vermont. "Checkerberry Corners" was formerly the name of a small post-office in Chittenden county, but the post-office department recently changed it to something considered more dignified, whether or not it was appropriate. It is sometimes termed partridge or

grouse-berry, in recognition of its food value to partridges and to other hibernating birds, but this name properly belongs to a still daintier creeping vine. The deer are also said to relish the fruit in autumn. It is always a pleasing plant to meet whether it is in late fall or early spring that one comes upon a bed of the polished, leathery, evergreen leaves and tempting red berries, sometimes two or three on a stem; or a little later, when the tender,

WINTERGREEN.
Flowers and fruit, × ½.

spicy, bronzed young sprigs are in evidence; or yet again in midsummer, when its dainty, drooping white flowers are half hidden under the foliage. These attractions combine to make it desirable for ornamental planting in borders and rockeries. The leaves were sometimes used as a substitute for tea during the Revolution; whence the name sometimes used, "mountain tea." Wintergreen oil is an agreeable aromatic product much used in flavoring confections and possessing mild medicinal properties. Ten pounds may be distilled from a ton of leaves. Much of the so-called wintergreen extract of the market is, however, obtained from the sweet birch.

CREEPING SNOWBERRY. *Chiogenes hispidula* (L.) T. & G. (*C. serpyllifolia* Salisb.)

This dainty little creeping plant is an evergreen, frequent in cool bogs and moist mossy woods. It is only slightly woody and so its place is doubtful in the present list. Its relationship to the wintergreen is evidenced by the like flavor of its leaf. Its dis-

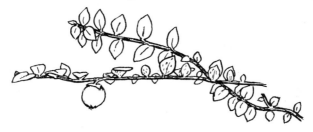

CREEPING SNOWBERRY.
Fruiting branch, natural size.

tinguishing characters are the very small leaves with margins rolled back, having rusty hairs below and also on the branches; its small nodding white flowers; and its snow-white, sweet, edible berries as large as small peas, ripening in late summer and autumn.

HUCKLEBERRY. *Gaylussacia baccata* (Wang.) Koch.

This shrub is familiar to all who have "gone blueberrying" in late July and August. It is a frequent plant on rocky hillsides and thickets, but thrives best in sandy or peat soil and so is often found in bogs. The leaves are easily distinguishable from the blueberries or other similar shrubs by their yellowish green tint above and the tiny resinous globules exuded from the lower surfaces. These give the underside of the young leaves a slightly rough, sticky feel and a glistening appearance if held in the sunlight. Later they may dry to a slight rusty scurf. The berries are sweet and of a peculiar flavor, preferred by many to that of the blueberries in spite of the fact that their seediness makes them objectionable. This seedy character, so evident between the teeth, probably accounts for its occasional name, crackleberry.　An-

HUCKLEBERRY.
Fruiting branch, × ½.

other, and in some sections, commoner name is whortleberry, said to come from the old Saxon heort-berg or hart's berry, from which our hurtleberry and huckleberry are in turn a corruption.　How much interesting history may be wrapped up in a homely name! The fruit of the huckleberry is one of the regular market berries of late summer.　It shows numerous varieties varying to blue (blue huckleberry) with a heavy bloom and with leaves either green on both sides or with a bluish bloom.　Various shades of scarlet and crimson develop in the autumn foliage of this plant and add an aesthetic charm to its commerciel value.

THE BLUEBERRIES.

There are some eight kinds of blueberry found in Vermont. Three of these, however, are rare, being practically confined to the alpine summits of the higher mountains; but the other five furnish fruit to the berry picker in one or another section of the state.　It will suffice the purpose of any except the mountain climbing botanist to distinguish these five as listed in the key below.　While none of these are cultivated for their fruit, large quantities of blueberries are gathered from the wild native plants. Attempts to cultivate blueberries have led to encouraging results in a few cases, the best returns being obtained with the common high-bush form[1].

---

[1] Anyone contemplating engaging in this industry should acquaint himself with the publications of Prof. W. M. Munson. See especially Me. Sta. Bul. 76 (1901).

THE COMMONER BLUEBERRIES.

1. High-bush forms, generally over 4 feet ....2.
1. Low-bush forms, generally less than 3 feet ....3.
2. Berries bluish-black with much bloom.
                                    Common high-bush blueberry.
2. Berries dead black without bloom......Black high-bush blueberry.
3. Branchlets and leaves downy..................Canada blueberry.
3. Branchlets and leaves smooth or nearly so ....4.
4. Leaves green and shining on both sides, distinctly but minutely
      toothed ....Early low blueberry.
4. Leaves pale or glaucous below, margins entire or sparingly
      toothed ....Late low blueberry.

COMMON HIGH-BUSH BLUEBERRY. *Vaccinium corymbosum* L.

This is the common tall or swamp blueberry frequenting the
low wet thickets over much of the state, and furnishing the
abundant late blueberry in the swamps about northern Lake

HIGHBUSH BLUEBERRY, × ⅔.

Champlain. It is a tall straggling shrub, typically five to ten
feet or even taller, but it varies quite widely in this and all other
characters. The branches are greenish brown with minute

brownish roughenings. Its leaf shape is shown in the drawing. It is typically about two inches long but may vary from one to three inches in length, entire and without hairs, the surface being green and smooth above, paler and often hairy below. A more pubescent form, green on both sides, occurs in some cold bogs (var. *amoenum*). The fruit is large, dark blue with bloom, ripens chiefly in late August. Its larger size and fine flavor make it the favorite market berry where obtainable. As already suggested it is easily transplanted, grows rapidly in any good soil and appears responsive to culture. It can be grafted if desired and doubtless, with improved varieties and cultural methods better understood, it will be added to our garden fruits.

BLACK BLUEBERRY. *Vaccinium atrococcum* (Gray) Heller.

This form is much like the high bush variety in most respects except that the fruit is smaller, black and without bloom. The leaves are downy or wooly underneath even when old, as are also the branchlets. It has been found in a few bogs but apparently is not common.

CANADA BLUEBERRY. *Vaccinium canadense* Kalm.

This is a low shrub one to two feet high, erect, densely branched, with young twigs yellowish-green and downy, older branches brownish. The leaf-form is shown in the figure. The best character whereby one may be able to identify this species is to be found in the downiness of its leaves and twigs. Because of this peculiarity the name velvet-leaf is often given to this blueberry. The berries are blue with much bloom and ripen rather late along with the common high-bush blueberry. It is frequent in the more elevated parts of Vermont, preferring moist thickets or rocky places, and is not found in swamps. It is said to be the commonest market berry of Essex county. The berries are of good flavor but more acid than are the common low-bush blueberry; hence the local name "sour-top" is sometimes heard.

They are also slightly smaller than are either the common low-bush or high-bush berries, but they are quite prolific. Their

Canada Blueberry, × ⅔.

smaller size and relative sourness make them less popular as market berries than are the others.

EARLY LOW BLUEBERRY. *Vaccinium pennsylvanicum* Lam.

This is a low or dwarf shrub of one to two feet in height. The slender branches are greenish, warty and generally smooth. The leaves are thin, small and narrow as shown in the figure and grade into the still smaller mountain variety (variety *angustifolium*) mentioned later. The fruit is typically bluish-black with bloom, but a form sometimes occurs having berries without bloom, (*nigrum*). It is the commonest berry on the low sandy plains and pine barrens and is frequent elsewhere in

dry sandy or rocky hillsides and open woodlands. The characters given in the key serve to distinguish it from the next named
form, but the important thing from the berry-pickers' standpoint is
that this is the earliest blueberry we have, ripening in late June
and July. It is extremely prolific and the berries are large, very
sweet and of fine flavor, making it the favorite early market
berry.   Indeed it supplies the bulk of the blueberries in all

EARLY LOW BLUEBERRY. × ⅔.

eastern markets. Although common in Vermont it is still more
plentiful in adjacent sections of northern New York and Canada, so that large quantities of berries from these points are
shipped into Vermont and to other and larger markets. When
mowed the new shoots produce the following year long spike-like
masses of bloom and fruit which may be stripped off by the hand-
ful. This species stands next to the high-bush berry in pos-
sibilities of cultivation and improvement.

LATE LOW BLUEBERRY. *Vaccinium vacillans* Kalm.

This is a low erect shrub, usually one to two feet but sometimes four feet high, common in dry sandy or rocky soils. Its branches are pale, yellowish green, warty, free from hairs; its

Late Low Blueberry, × ⅔.

leaves are distinguishable from those of the early low form, as
shown in the key and the accompanying cut, by being larger and
broader, smooth with entire margins, pale green above and
whiter underneath. The fruit is a large blue berry with much
bloom and excellent flavor. It ripens in July and August along
with the late high berries and so contributes a part of the later
market berries. It deserves the attention of anyone attempting
blueberry culture, though it is not so promising as the two previously commended.

THE MOUNTAIN BLUEBERRIES.

Anyone visiting the higher mountain summits, especially
Mansfield, in midsummer may find the following three mountain
blueberries. All are dwarfs, but a few inches in height, matted
in the moss of boggy depressions along with the bearberry and
mountain cranberry. The fruits of all are sweet and edible.

The narrow-leaved variety of the early dwarf blueberry already described (*V. pennsylvanicum* var. *angustifolium* Gray)
is found on Mansfield and Camel's Hump, only a few inches in
height and with narrower and lanceolate, minutely-toothed leaves,
and berries bluish-black with bloom.

The bog bilberry, (*V. uliginosum* L.) forms low tufts with
the preceding and has been found at lower altitudes. It is
characterized by the shorter rounded leaves with an entire margin, which show a dull bluish cast above, and are paler and
slightly pubescent beneath. The fruit is blue-black with bloom.

The dwarf bilberry (*V. caespitosum* Michx) completes the
arctic trio. Its leaves are larger than those of either of the others,
minutely toothed, yellow green, smooth and shining on both
sides. Its berries are larger and blue with bloom. This is at
home on "the chin," the highest point of Mount Mansfield, but
has also been located in Newfane and Washington.

THE CRANBERRIES.

It may surprise some to learn that there are at least three kinds of cranberry native to Vermont. Since all are edible, and one of them is the same as the species so profitably cultivated in Massachusetts and New Jersey, it leads one to question why more has not been done with cranberry growing in Vermont. There is no reason apparent why cranberry bogs might not be successfully established at many places in the state. Indeed this has been done by several parties in years past. The native cranberries all have low creeping stems, small evergreen leaves and red berries. The species are distinguished as follows:

1. Underside of leaves green and dotted with blackish, bristly points ....Mountain cranberry.
1. Underside of leaves whitened and smooth ....2.
2. Leaves acute-pointed, margins rolled strongly backward (revolute) ....Small cranberry.
2. Leaves obtuse pointed, margins less revolute......Large cranberry.

LARGE CRANBERRY. *Vaccinium macrocarpon* Ait.

The large or American cranberry is cultivated in Massachusetts, especially at Cape Cod, in New Jersey and Wisconsin. The cut shows leaf and fruit relations well. The berries

are usually spherical or somewhat elongated, red when ripe, one-half inch more or less in diameter, and of characteristic acid flavor. The fruit even in the wild state varies considerably in color and outline, and under culture several such varieties have been developed and named. It is peculiarly an American fruit but has already found a large market abroad. The plant is frequent as a native in peat bogs,

LARGE CRANBERRY, × ½.   open swamps, or wet shores at

the lower altitudes.   It seems to prefer grassy swamps or sandy bogs. The stems are slender, prostrate, one to four feet long, rooting at the joints and throwing up erect branches a few inches in height upon which the flowers and fruits are borne.   It is stated on good authority that cranberry culture will nearly always prove successful on bogs where the berry is native, providing certain conditions can be complied with.   Chief among these are:

    1.   A level surface capable of drainage;

    2.   Abundance of clean sand;

    3.   An ample supply of water which can at need be held in storage. The flooding of the bog at will is necessary for winter protection, spring retardation, and possible use in summer and autumn against injurious pests or early frost.

SMALL CRANBERRY. *Vaccinium oxycoccus* L.

The stem of this species is shorter and more slender than that of the larger one just described, but its habit of growth is in other respects quite similar.   The difference in leaf character is made clear by the key on the preceding page.   The fruit is only about one half the diameter of the larger species, reddish and often speckled with white when young.   The flavor is similar to that of the large berry and is preferred by some.   It is a sub-arctic plant often found in Vermont in cold peat bogs. It is collected and used, when in sufficient quantity, and is even offered occasionally in the Vermont markets.   This is the cranberry of the old world, large quantities being supplied from Russia to the south of Europe.   A variety of this species (var. *intermedium* Gray) occurs occasionally which is intermediate in leaf and fruit characters between this and the large cranberry.

MOUNTAIN CRANBERRY. *Vaccinium vitis-idaea* L. var. *minus* Lodd.

This species is also known as the cowberry and foxberry. It is a mountain species found in Vermont only on the summits of

Mansfield and Camel's Hump. There it is abundant enough so that the berries are often gathered for sauce by summer visitors. They are about the size of the small cranberry, dark red, and rather bitter when uncooked. It is abundant in sections of Canada where it is used in the homes and offered in some markets. The habit of the vine is similar to that of the other cranberries, but its branches are shorter and its leaves larger, leathery, and of a glossy, dark green. It is recommended for planting in ornamental borders.

WILD ROSEMARY. *Andromeda glaucophylla* Link. (*A. polifolia* L.)

The wild rosemary or water andromeda is a bush one to three feet high, frequently found in wet, peaty soil, especially bordering bogs and boggy ponds. It has red flower buds which expand into small white or pinkish flowers, nodding in clusters at the ends of the branches, followed by dry globular capsules. The characters most surely recognizable pertain to the leaves, which are narrow—about one-fourth by two inches—with margins strongly recurved, white beneath, evergreen and thick. They are somewhat acrid and contain a narcotic poison which is said to prove fatal to browsing sheep.

WILD ROSEMARY.
In flower, × ⅔.

MALE BERRY. *Lyonia ligustrina* (L) DC. (*Andromeda Xolisma*).

This is occasional in southern Vermont in damp woodlands. It is a deciduous shrub three to ten feet high. The small white blossoms are borne in many-flowered terminal clusters which are often several inches long.

LEATHER LEAF. *Chamaedaphne calyculata* (L.) Moench.
(*Cassandra*).

This species is closely allied to the preceding shrubs. It favorite habitat, also, is wet places and it is frequent in boggy

meadows and swamp borders. It grows two to four feet high and spreads by suckers which enable it to form large beds. The leaves are evergreen, leathery in texture, covered on both sides, but more densely below, with minute, roundish, scurvy scales. Those of the upper surface are whitish and appear to the naked eye as tiny white specks; on the lower surface they are brown and give this side a rusty appearance. The egg-shaped flowers appear in early spring, hanging like rows of tiny white bells from the undersides of the younger twigs.

LEATHER-LEAF.
In flower, × ½.

It is one of the shrubs which make the swamps attractive to the nature lover.

TRAILING ARBUTUS. *Epigaea repens* L.

Everyone knows the arbutus or mayflower. Emerson says of its occurrence in Massachusetts, "Often from beneath the edge of a snowbank are seen rising the fragrant, pearly-white or rose-colored, crowded flowers of this earliest harbinger of spring. It abounds in the edges of the woods about Plymouth, as elsewhere, and must have been the first to salute the storm-beaten crew of the Mayflower on the conclusion of their first terrible winter. Their descendants have thence piously derived the name, although its bloom is often found before the coming of the month

of May." The flower buds are formed the preceding summer
and so are ready to swell with the first premonitions of spring.
The arbutus is common in certain regions, preferring sandy soil;
and its growth is sparse wherever such soil conditions are lacking. Those gathering it should realize that its shrubby stems

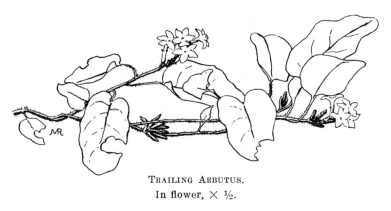

TRAILING ARBUTUS.
In flower, × ½.

are of relatively slow growth, and that their normal development
is conditioned on their lying as they naturally do, close to the soil.
Wherever there is danger of its extermination, therefore, the
flower clusters should be cut without disturbing these stems un-
necessarily. A notice stating this fact has been prepared by the
Society for the Protection of Native Plants. A copy of it may
be secured for posting in any school room or other suitable
place by addressing the secretary of that society at the Library
of the Boston Society of Natural History.

THE LAUREL.   KALMIA.

The name "laurel" most properly belongs to a European
plant as noted under the laurel family on an earlier page. In
this country it has been applied rather indiscriminately to several
others. The kalmias however by popular usage are denominated
as the American laurels, the large rhododendron alone having
claims that rival them. And this group of plants, for the kalmias

and rhododendrons are closely allied, are well worthy the distinction, so preeminent are they for richness of evergreen foliage as well as for flower. Vermont boasts three species of kalmia. In passing it is worthy of note that Linneaus chose this rather curious name in honor of his pupil, Peter Kalm, who was sent to America as a botanical explorer by the Royal Academy of Sweden in 1748. He spent some weeks in the Champlain valley, carrying many plants back to Europe for study and naming. He was doubtless the first botanist to visit Vermont. Among other things he recorded the fact that the young sheep of the early colonists browsing in winter upon the evergreen leaves of the laurel were fatally poisoned and that other stock were made very sick. Kalm's observations were made especially on the mountain laurel. Later records showed the sheep laurel to be similarly poisonous. It has also been shown that honey made from these two plants is poisonous, and it is claimed by some that when partridges feed on the buds their flesh is rendered unwholesome. The flowers of all the kalmias are curious and interesting. They are saucer-shaped with their stamens bent backward and anthers concealed until maturity in pockets in the corolla. When the blossom is fully open and these are touched by a visiting insect they are released and with a spring-like action dust pollen over the visitor's body, thus insuring cross-pollination. Someone has compared them in form to miniature parasols, the corolla to the cover, the reflexed stamens to the ribs, and the central style to the handle. The illustrations, especially of the mountain laurel, will help to make these points clearer, but they need to be seen in a fresh blossom if one is fully to appreciate their beauty.

1. Leaves bright green both sides, relatively broad, i. e. one inch or more wide by two to three long........Mountain laurel.
1. Leaves paler or whitish underneath, relatively narrow, i. e. one-half inch or less wide ....2.
2. Leaves with margins rolled strongly backward, white underneath, flower clusters at end of branch..........Pale laurel.
2. Leaves not so rolled or white underneath, flower clusters along side of branch with young leafy shoots at end..Sheep laurel.

SHEEP LAUREL. *Kalmia angustifolia* L.

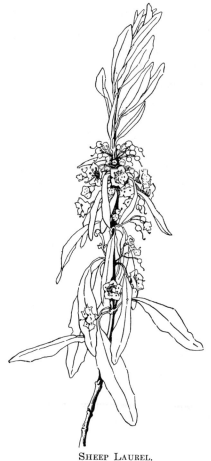

The sheep laurel is the commonest of the three species, being an erect shrub one to three feet high, forming patches on hillsides and in low moist sandy soil. It is rather unattractive with its somewhat drooping foliage until the bright purplish flowers appear. Even then it is Cinderella of the trio. Its reputation as a poison to sheep is witnessed in its common names, sheep laurel and lambkill, and it is held by some to be even more poisonous to stock than is the broad-leaved laurel.

SHEEP LAUREL.
In flower, × ½.

PALE LAUREL. *Kalmia polifolia* Wang. (*K. glauca* Ait.)

This is a small straggling shrub about one foot high which occurs occasionally in cold peat bogs. It is well characterized by the leaves, dark green above, whitish beneath, with margins rolled back. The twigs also are peculiar in being two-edged. The flowers are showy, lilac-purple, one-half inch in diameter. They form showy clusters making the plant conspicuous and attractive when in flower about the first of June.

MOUNTAIN LAUREL. *Kalmia latifolia* L.

This most beautiful shrub is the laurel of southern New England, but in Vermont, unfortunately, it occurs native only in southern valleys. It is known by a variety of popular names; broad-leaved laurel, to contrast it with the other two; calico-bush, from its showy rose and white blossoms; spoonwood, from the use of its wood by the Indians for carving into spoons. Clamoun was the Indian name. The poisonous nature of this plant has already been discussed; fortunately, however, where its character is understood this is easily guarded against, hence there is no necessity to wage war on this beautiful plant. On the other hand, since it is easily transplanted, it deserves to be used far more than it is as an ornamental shrub.

LABRADOR TEA. *Ledum groenlandicum* Oed.

LABRADOR TEA.
Flowering branch, × ⅔.

This is a straggling, branching shrub of one to four feet in height. It is of frequent occurrence in Vermont in cold peaty bogs and wet mountain woods, preferring sandy soil. It is typically a northern plant as witnessed by its name. It has most curious leaves, thick and leathery with margins rolled strongly backward, dark green above and densely covered below with woolly hair which may be white on the youngest shoots but is rusty brown on the mature leaves. Since these hairs are nature's device to check the loss of water, it seems strange that a bog plant should be provided with them. The flowers are white about one-third of an inch across, forming a rather showy cluster at the end of the branch in early summer. The leaves are rich in tannin and possess some narcotic principle. They are used for tanning in Russia. In Labrador a decoction of the leaves is sometimes drunk as a tea, whence the name. It is said, though we cannot vouch for the authority, that it was also so used in the American colonies· during the Revolution.

AZALEA. RHODODENDRON.

These names suggest our most showy flowering shrubs. There are three species in Vermont, all worth looking for but none common. The flowers of the rhododendrons are very showy, slightly irregular and with the curved stamens extruded. All the native rhododendrons are worthy of culture. This offers no difficulty providing that they are planted in moist peaty soil such as abounds naturally or is easily prepared.

1. Leaves evergreen and large (two by five inches or more).
                                                      Great rhododendron.
1. Leaves deciduous and smaller (one by two inches or less).......2
2. Leaves about one-half as wide as long, petals united for one-
     half their length into a tube; stamens usually 5.
                                                      Pink azalea.
2. Leaves about one-third as wide as long, petals almost distinct;
     stamens 10 ....Rhodora.

GREAT RHODODENDRON. *Rhododendron maximum* L.

This is known to occur in only a few places in northeastern Vermont, about the shores of Groton and neighboring ponds. It is there a low spreading plant of three to six feet with the lower branches semi-prostrate. The fully developed leaves are from four to six inches or more in length and one-fourth as wide. They are thick, smooth and leathery, on thick leaf-stalks, evergreen and persistent or several year. The flowers open about July 1. They form in large clusters at the ends of the shoots, are about one and one-half inches across and of somewhat variable pale-rose tints sprinkled with yellowish or reddish dots. It is the most showy of our native flowering shrubs and is one of the most beautiful of all native flowers. It is often cultivated as an ornamental plant, but the stock in these cases is usually obtained through nurserymen from the Alleghany mountains, where it is much more abundant. It deserves much wider use than has been made of it as yet in Vermont.

PINK AZALEA. *Rhododendron canescens* (Mx.) G. Don.

This shrub is more widely distributed in Vermont than is the rhododendron proper, but it is found only occasionally growing in moist, woody banks and along the borders of swamps. It is sometimes called swamp-pink, June pink, honeysuckle, or pinxter-flower, the first of these names being commonest in

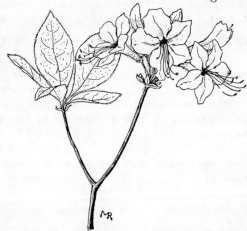

PINK AZALEA, × ½.

local usage in Vermont. The name "may-apple" is sometimes given it because of the large apple-like galls which are common on the twigs. It is a low spreading shrub rarely more than a few feet in height, with oval, deciduous and more or less hairy leaves. The flowers opening the last of May are pink of varying shades, spreading to an inch and a half or more in width and are decidedly cinnamon scented. They have not the delicacy of color of the flowers of the true rhododendron, but the plant excels it in grace and merits more attention than has yet been given it for ornamental planting.

RHODORA. *Rhododendron canadense* (L.) B S. P. (*R. rhodora* L.)

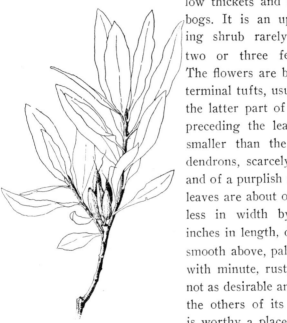

This also is a swamp-loving plant found occasionally in low thickets and bordering cool bogs. It is an upright branching shrub rarely rising above two or three feet in height. The flowers are borne in showy terminal tufts, usually appearing the latter part of May and just preceding the leaves. They are smaller than the other rhododendrons, scarcely an inch long and of a purplish rose color. The leaves are about one-half inch or less in width by one to two inches in length, dark green and smooth above, paler beneath and with minute, rusty hairs. While not as desirable an ornamental as the others of its class, rhodora is worthy a place in the garden of any one fond of hardy, native, ornamental shrubs.

RHODORA.
Branch with fruit capsules, × ½.

OLIVE FAMILY. OLEACEAE

The ash is our only native representative of this family of trees and shrubs. Since all of the ashes are trees they were discussed in "Trees of Vermont." Several of the shrubby species are introduced in cultivation, including the privets (*Ligustrum*), the fringe-tree (*Chionanthus*), and forsythia with its golden bells in earliest spring. More common almost than the ashes are the lilacs, and these are indeed so frequent and persistent as to deserve a place in any list of Vermont shrubs. The common purple and white varieties belong to one European species (*S. vulgaris*). The daintier persian lilac is also frequently seen, and occasionally the less attractive josika lilac, as well as others.

NIGHTSHADE FAMILY. SOLANACEAE

The word nightshade has an unsavory sound to most people. While there are numerous poisonous plants among its members, the deadly nightshade is largely the creation of the poet's fancy. The cultivated tomato and potato are witnesses of the economic worth of some of the group and there are several other members much prized as garden vegetables or ornamental plants. On the other hand the European belladonna and the common wild nightshades of this country, especially the black nightshade, have poisonous properties. Testimony differs, however, as to the toxic effects of the black nightshade. Its berries are sometimes and in some sections eaten with impunity, whereas in other cases serious illness and even death has resulted from their ingestion. It is possible that variations in individual susceptibilities as to their solanin content, or, indeed, differences in such content due to varying conditions of growth, may account for these diverse observations. However, the only safe procedure is to treat the nightshades as poisonous plants and especially to warn children against eating the berries.

CLIMBING NIGHTSHADE. *Solanum dulcamara* L..

This is a common vine in moist thickets, sometimes actually growing in the water, at other times in relatively dry soil, as along fence rows. It is also called bittersweet, but this name is confusing since it is applied to another vine, the celastrus described earlier. It is listed as an introduced plant, but it is now so widely distributed as at least to appear like a native. It is a perennial plant with weak stem, more or less woody at the base but herbaceous above, clambering upon other shrubs or

over old fences and stones. The leaves are curiously variable
in shape and size. The purplish flowers resemble potato blossoms. The red berries are egg-shaped, about the size of large
currants, borne in clusters which become conspicuous and beau-

CLIMBING NIGHTSHADE.
Branch with flower and fruit, × ⅓.

tiful as they ripen in the autumn. The plant has medicinal
properties and was formerly used as an herb remedy in Europe.
The name bittersweet probably arose from the fact, as stated
by Lindley, that in England the young stems collected in the autumn for medicinal purposes "have at first a bitter taste which
is succeeded by an agreeable sweetness." The berries yield
green and violet dyes. The climbing nightshade is sufficiently
attractive so that it is planted as an ornamental vine to cover
low banks and trellises. For most places preferable plants can
be found, unless this is introduced for variety's sake.

MADDER FAMILY. RUBIACEAE

This large family of plants includes several of much economic interest such as madder and other dye plants, the ipecac

plant, the cinchonas which are the source of Peruvian bark, and the coffee plant.   There are numerous Vermont herbaceous plants including the cleavers and bluet, but only one shrub.

BUTTON-BUSH.   *Cephalanthus occidentalis* L.

This is a shrub, usually four to ten feet high, forming thickets commonly in open swamps and along low shores of ponds and streams. It is easily known by the spherical clusters of small white blossoms forming ball-like heads an inch or more in diameter. The greenish heads of fruit which follow the blossoms are also ball-shaped. The large shiny leaves, which add to the plant's attractiveness, are in pairs or threes, and have entire margins and a somewhat leathery texture.   The tincture of the bark has been used somewhat as a medicine, but the plant is chiefly to be prized for its ornamental qualities, whether as it occurs in nature or as transplanted. It does quite as well on drier soil and has to recommend it, bright foliage and especially the fact that the curious and attractive flowering balls appear during midsummer when few other shrubs are in bloom.

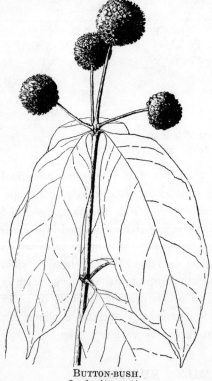

BUTTON-BUSH.
In fruit, × ½.

HONEYSUCKLE FAMILY. CAPRIFOLIACEAE

This family is to be rated with the cornels, heaths and roses as a source of ornamental shrubs. Nearly all of the Vermont species are shrubs. Some of them furnish dyes and medicines of minor value, but it is chiefly for the beauty of foliage, flower and fruit that they are valued. All are attractive in nature and most of them are used for landscape planting. The family characters are shown in the opposite leaves, rather conspicuous and often irregular flowers, and berry-formed fruit. The six genera are distinguishable as follows:

1. Flowers in broad, compound clusters ....5.
1. Flowers solitary in pairs, or in narrow clusters.................2.
2. A creeping vine ....Twinflower.
2. Upright or climbing shrub ....3.
3. Fruit a dry capsule ....Bush honeysuckle.
3. Fruit a fleshy berry ....4.
4. Berry white, only 2-seeded ....Snowberry.
4. Berries colored, several seeded ....Loniceras.
5. Leaves compound ....Elders.
5. Leaves simple ....Virburnums.

TWIN-FLOWER. *Linnaea borealis* L. var. *americana* (Forbes) Rehder.

This daintiest of trailing plants occurs occasionally in moist, mossy woods especially under evergreens. It is found in northern Europe as well as America and was named for the great Swedish botanist, Linnaeus, with whom it was an especial favorite. It has a slender, woody stem which may creep for several feet beneath the surface of the moss and humus. From this, short stems arise which bear the small round leaves in pairs and, near the summit, slender flower stalks two or three inches high, forking at the top to support the two delicate fragrant, nodding, rose-tinted flowers.

BUSH-HONEYSUCKLE. *Diervilla lonicera* Mill. (*D. trifida* Moench)

This is a modest little shrub, two to three feet high, spreading from the root so as to form groups, bordering woodlands

and roadside thickets. The leaves are opposite, rather sharply
toothed and with a long tapering point, four delicate ridges con-
necting the leaf bases, giving a somewhat four-sided appearance.
The flowers which open in June and July are honey-yellow, about

BUSH HONEYSUCKLE.
Fruiting branch, × ½.

three-fourths inch long, in small clusters, most commonly of
three, arising from the leaf axils near the ends of the stem. These
are closely related to the handsome Japanese shrub weigela, which
is much cultivated for ornament.   Our little native has but slight
claim for such purpose although it is attractive in its wild state.

SNOWBERRY.   *Symphoricarpos racemosus* Michx.

This is a low spreading shrub, usually less than one foot
high, found on the cliffs and headlands of western Vermont. It
has small roundish leaves, about one inch long, and bears two or
three flowers in a cluster in the uppermost leaf axils from which
ripen waxy white berries of the size of peas. The snowberry or
waxberry often cultivated as an ornamental plant is a larger
variety of the same species, (var. *laevigatus*), not native of Ver-

mont but becoming frequent as an escape from cultivation. It resembles its smaller relative save that it is taller, being from

SNOWBERRY.
In fruit, × ½.

two to six feet in height, and that it bears larger leaves and more numerous flowers and fruits. It is, however, best distinguished by the fact that the native species has leaves which are velvety-hairy beneath, whereas the garden variety is without hairs. Some medicinal worth is attributed to the berries.

HONEYSUCKLE.   LONICERA.

This is a group of six shrubs, five natives and one common in old gardens and as an escape. They are characterized, as explained in the key, by their colored and several-seeded berries. The leaves are in all cases opposite, with entire margins, and the flowers are as a rule rather showy and fragrant.

1. Stems twining, flowers in small terminal clusters, uppermost leaves united at the base ....2.
1. Upright, bushy shrubs with leaves all distinct, flowers in pairs..3.
2. Branches and leaves smooth, whitened (glaucous) beneath.
                                        Glaucous honeysuckle.
2. Branches and leaves downy-hairy............Hairy honeysuckle.
3. The flower stem shorter than the flowers, berry double, blue.
                                        Blue honeysuckle.
3. The flowers on a distinct stem as long or longer than the flowers; berries reddish or yellow ....4.
4. Tall shrubs (five to fifteen feet) cultivated or escaped.
                                        Tartarian honeysuckle.
4. Small shrubs (two to five feet) native ....5.
5. Blossoms in May, berries red, single...........Fly honeysuckle.
5. Blossoms in June, berries purplish, more or less doubled.
                                        Swamp honeysuckle.

GLAUCOUS HONEYSUCKLE. *Lonicera dioica* L. (*L. glauca* Hill).

This species frequents rocky woodlands preferring dry to moist soils. It has a weakly stem, usually three to six feet long, but capable of developing somewhat of a shrubby habit in the absence of other support. It is a plant of such unusual appearance

GLAUCOUS HONEYSUCKLE.
Branch with clusters of berries, × ½.

as to attract attention. The stems are a light gray; the leaves are large, smooth, whitish (glaucous) beneath, the upper ones curiously united in pairs at the base; the greenish yellow or purplish flowers are nearly one-third of an inch long, a half dozen or so in a compact terminal cluster, followed by a crowded cluster of reddish berries, the size of peas. It is sometimes cultivated as an ornamental plant and deserves attention where a covering is desired for a wall or rock work.

HAIRY HONEYSUCKLE. *Lonicera hirsuta* Eaton.

This occurs only occasionally in the rocky woodlands of western Vermont. It is much like the preceding species in twining habit and general characters. It is, however, a coarser plant with larger leaves, flowers and fruit, and is easily distinguished by the downy-hairiness of the shoots and leaves, especially underneath.

BLUE HONEYSUCKLE. *Lonicera caerulea* L. var. *villosa* (Mx.) T. & G.

This is a low shrub, one or two feet in height, found occasionally in the cold bogs of northeastern Vermont. It may be readily distinguished from either of the preceding species, but is very similar to the next one. The leaves in both are small with short stems and are rounded at the base. The short flower stem and the double blue berry are, however, characteristic, as explained in the key.

SWAMP HONEYSUCKLE. *Lonicera oblongifolia* (Goldie) Hook.

This is found in a few of the cold, swampy bogs of the state. It is a larger shrub, two to five feet high, similar to the preceding species as well as to the one that follows. It is distinguishable from the blue honeysuckle, as explained in the key, by the longer flower stem and the purplish and more or less united berries, and from the fly honeysuckle by the marked differences in the fruit as indicated in the key on page 179.

FLY HONEYSUCKLE. *Lonicera canadensis* Marsh. (*L. ciliata* Muhl.)

This is a shrub, three to five feet in height with straggling branches, common in moist thickets and woodlands. The flowers are greenish-yellow, three-fourths of an inch long and borne in pairs on slender stalks which are usually about half the length of the leaves. The berries also are in pairs, about one-fourth of an inch long, egg-shaped and red when ripe. It is the commonest Vermont lonicera and ordinarily apt to be confused only with the

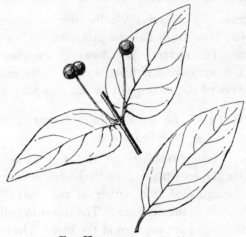

FLY HONEYSUCKLE, × ½.

diervilla or bush honeysuckle, which is easily recognized by its toothed, long-pointed leaf as well as by its fruit, an elongated dry capsule. It is not so easy, however, to differentiate the fly honeysuckle from the swamp honeysuckle. The latter will rarely be found and then only in cold swamps. The fly honeysuckle has a longer petiole, with leaves broader and often heart shaped at the base, shorter flower stalks and separate red berries. The fly honeysuckle is sometimes used for ornamental planting, though hardly equal for this purpose to the bush honeysuckle.

TARTARIAN HONEYSUCKLE. *Lonicera tartarica* L.

This is perhaps, next to the lilacs, the commonest shrub planted for ornament in Vermont. Probably through the agency of the birds, seedlings have sprung up frequently by fence rows and in waste places, sometimes appearing as if native. It is a vigorous, long-lived shrub of about the size and general habit of the lilac but with smaller leaves and branches. It well merits its place in popular favor because of its hardiness in all situations, its wealth of fragrant bloom and its loads of scarcely less attractive berries. It varies widely in color of flower and fruit.

TARTARIAN HONEYSUCKLE.
Flowering branch, $\times$ ½.

Some bushes bear creamy white, others deep pink or rose hued blossoms. The color of the berries varies with that of the flower, the white blossoms giving lighter yellow fruit, the darker flower tints being associated with a coral-red berry. The leaves vary in like relation from a lighter to a darker green.

THE ELDERS. SAMBUCUS.

The elders are so familiar as scarcely to require description. There is however frequent confusion of the name elder and alder. Both are so common that it is only necessary to recall that the alder has simple rounded leaves and dry cone-like fruits, whereas the elders have large compound leaves and blue or red berries. This distinction is well emphasized in the common name elderberry. The two species of elder are common and both are rather coarse with a penetrating odor when bruised or cut. The leaves are large, opposite and compound with the leaflets toothed. The

flowers are somewhat fragrant, white and rather small, but are
borne in large showy masses. These, appearing in the earlier
species in late spring and in the others in early summer, are
followed in turn by the ample and richly colored fruit clusters,
the one in midsummer and the other in autumn. These characteristics combine to make the elders surpass all other native
shrubs in giving large and pleasing color effects to our waysides. The two elders are distinguished as follows:

Flowers in broad flat clusters in June, fruit dark purple, pith white.
Common elder.
Flower clusters pyramidal in May, fruit red, pith brown.
Red-berried elder.

COMMON ELDER. *Sambucus canadensis* L.

The common elder is a shrub usually five to ten feet high,
which is fond of rich moist soil and plenty of sunlight, thriving in
wayside thickets where its quick-growing stems soon overtop
the blackberries and vie with the dogwoods. The ample flower
clusters open in June and July, just when most needed to add
color to the waysides; the black-purple berries ripen in September. An English botanist, Smith, says that the "uncertain summer is established when the elder is in full flower and is entirely
gone when its berries are ripe." The elder has been made useful in various ways. Emerson summarizes these as follows:
"An infusion of the juice of the berries is a delicate test for acids
and alkalies; an infusion of the bruised leaves is used by garden-
ers to expel insects from vines; a wholesome sudorific tea is
made from the flowers; the unopened flower buds when pickled
make an excellent substitute for capers; the abundant pith is the
best substance for the pith balls used in electrical experiments;
and the hollow shoots are in great use with boys for popguns
and fifes." To this of course must be added the use of the ripe
berries, much more common formerly than now, for elderberry
wine. They were even made into pies, but there is no need of
such usage to-day in view of the abundance of better fruit.

Common Elder.
In flower, × ½.

RED-BERRIED ELDER.   *Sambucus racemosa* L.

This is a smaller bush than the preceding, three to seven
feet being its general range of height.   The stem is more woody
than that of the common elder, and the leaflets are downy underneath instead of being smooth.   Otherwise the two species
bear a general resemblance in stem and leaf characters, but

RED-BERRIED ELDER.
Fruiting branch, × ½.

the difference between the two is well marked in both flower and
fruit as indicated in the key above.   The red berries ripening in
June form a striking contrast to the green foliage and they
are soon stripped off by the birds.   The berries are not poisonous as is sometimes claimed, but they are repugnant to the taste
and no use is made of them.   Nearly all parts of the plant have
been used in compounding herb medicines, but to-day the flower
buds alone are recognized by the pharmacopea as of medicinal
value.

ARROW-WOOD FAMILY. VIBURNUM

Several species of these common and attractive shrubs have high value for ornamental planting. They have opposite leaves, white flowers, usually in rather showy flat clusters, in some cases the marginal ones being larger, and conspicuous red or bluish berries. In noting the color of the fruit, however, it should be remembered that this often passes through intermediate reddish stages before reaching its mature color. The arrow-woods are often confused with the dogwoods from which they are distinguished by the fact that the berry contains one flattened stony seed, whereas the dogwood berries have an oval, two-celled, two-seeded stone. All the dogwoods have entire leaves whereas nearly all the viburnums have leaves more or less toothed or lobed. The name arrow-wood suggests the fact that the Indians found the straight shoots of some of these shrubs serviceable for arrow shafts.

1. Flower clusters with some marginal flowers much larger than the rest; mature fruit red 2
1. Flowers all of same size in cluster; mature fruit generally blue black (red under 4) 3
2. Leaves with three to five heavy veins radiating from the base (palmate); coarsely 3-lobed ....High cranberry-bush.
2. Leaves with 1 midrib (pinnate); finely toothed.....Hobble-bush.
3. Leaves with three to five heavy veins radiating from the base (palmate); usually more or less 3-lobed 4
3. Leaves with 1 midrib (pinnate); never lobed 5
4. Leaves soft-downy beneath; flower clusters one and one-half to two inches wide, terminal, mature berries blue-black.
                                        Maple-leaved arrow-wood.
4. Leaves nearly or quite smooth beneath; flower clusters one-half to one inch wide, lateral; mature berries red.
                                        Few-flowered cranberry-bush.
5. Leaves coarsely toothed 6
5. Leaves finely toothed or entire 7
6. Leaf-stalks (petioles) downy and very short (less than one-fourth inch) leaves velvety-downy especially underneath.
                                        Downy arrow-wood.

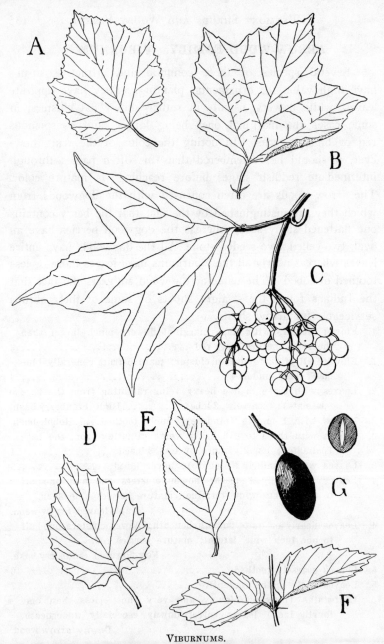

VIBURNUMS.

A, Few-flowered Cranberry-bush; B, Maple-leaved Arrow-wood; C,
High Cranberry-bush; D, Toothed Arrow-wood; E, Withe-rod; F,
Downy Arrow-wood; G, Sheep-berry (surface and in section).
A-F are × ½, G is natural size.

6. Leaf-stalks smooth and longer (one-half inch or more; leaves
smooth except for some hairs about base and angles of veins
underneath ....Toothed arrow-wood.

7. Leaves with long-tapering acute apex and sharply-toothed margins; mature berries one-half inch or more long..Sheep-berry.

7. Leaves with rounded or obtuse pointed apex; margins dull-
toothed or entire; berries one-fourth inch long....Withe-rod.

HIGH CRANBERRY-BUSH. *Viburnum opulus* L. var. *americanum* (Mill.) Ait.

This plant has an upright bushy habit and is from five to ten
feet in height. It is scattered through swamps and low moist
woodlands, especially along streams but, if transplanted, will
grow well in dry soil. It is rendered conspicuous by flower, fruit
and leaf. The leaves are strongly three-lobed, usually with
spreading lobe-tips. The blossoms open in May or early June in
clusters three to four inches across, rendered showy by the large
white marginal flowers, one-half inch or more in diameter. The
berries pass from a green through yellowish tints to a bright red
in ripening and are not only showy during the autumn but may
cling to the branches through the winter. They have a single
large flat stone, a pleasant acid flavor similar to that of the true
cranberry and are sometimes used as a substitute for it in sauce
and pastry. Some medicinal properties are attributed to this plant.
The native shrub is frequently used for ornamental planting and
well deserves usage. The common snowball-bush or guelder-rose,
so much grown for ornament, is a horticultural variety of this
same species, but is of European ancestry. It differs only in
having all the flowers of the cluster showy and sterile and hence
forms no fruit.

FEW-FLOWERED CRANBERRY-BUSH. *Viburnum pauciflorum* Raf.

This is a sub-alpine species closely allied to the last. It is a
low straggling shrub, two to four feet in height, found only on
the two higher mountains, Mansfield and Killington, in the

moist ravines near the limit of tree growth. No one need confuse it, therefore, with either of the species of lower altitudes.
If there is doubt, the characters mentioned in the preceding key
will suffice for its recognition. The berries are acid and edible
though too rare to be of practical use.

HOBBLE-BUSH. *Viburnum alnifolium* Marsh.

This is also called wayfaring-tree, a name first given to an
English relative. Emerson, commenting on the origin of this
curious name, quotes the English poet Howitt:

"Wayfaring tree! What ancient claim
Hast thou to that right pleasant name?
....
What'er it be, I love it well;
A name methinks, that surely fell
From poet, in some evening dell,
Wandering with fancies sweet."

Hobble-bush is a name, the origin of which is quite vague.
Possibly it originated from the fact that the low horizontal branches near the ground cause one to trip frequently.

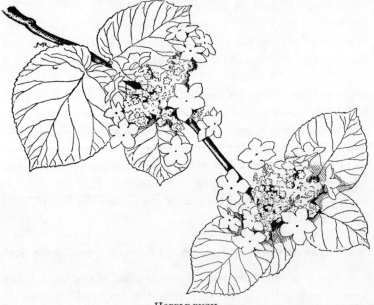

HOBBLE-BUSH.
Flowering branch, × ⅓.

However, this plant is one that must be known by some name to every lover of Vermont's mountain roads. It is a low irregular shrub rising usually but a few inches from the ground. Often its forking branches are nearly or quite prostrate and, striking root, start new colonies. The leaves are few but large and unusually attractive, from the time they burst their rusty buds in spring. through their sturdy summer development to a size of four to to six inches, with dark green colors traced with the delicate network of veins, until they end with the rich reds and browns of autumn. The buds are conspicuous and attractive in winter. The blossoms, too, stand out in large clusters bordered with the larger sterile marginal flowers which are often an inch across. The rusty brown hairs coating the young shoots, flower and leaf stalks and the lower leaf surface add to the color effect, and these are still further heightened by the berries ripening from red to a rich purplish-black. They are not edible. The hobble-bush deserves a place in ornamental plantations in any cool, moist situation, but nowhere can it be so charming as when fringing a trout brook on the mountain side.

MAPLE-LEAVED ARROW-WOOD.   *Viburnum acerifolium* L.

This is a low, erect shrub of three to five feet, frequently found in rocky woodlands. The leaves bear a close resemblance to the common red maple in outline, which is the more striking since both plants have opposite leaves. Closer attention suffices to remove any doubt as between these, however, since the arrow-wood leaves, .especially the younger ones, are so soft-hairy beneath as to be velvety to the touch, whereas the maple leaf is smooth. The arrow-wood also flowers and fruits freely and so shows its family characters. The berries are blue-black when ripe and of disagreeable taste. This is a desirable small shrub for ornamental planting, its value being enhanced by the attractive purple hues of its autumn foliage. The name Dockmakie, probably of Indian origin, is sometimes applied to it.

DOWNY ARROW-WOOD. *Viburnum pubescens* (Ait.) Pursh.

This is a low straggling shrub with slender branches two to five feet high. It is frequent in the Champlain valley, preferring dry rocky woodlands. It is sometimes used in ornamental plantings and is to be recommended especially for dry, partially shaded banks. Its natural habitat in dry woods segregates it in nature from the next species which it most closely resembles. If, however, the two are intermingled the characters emphasized in the key will suffice to distinguish them.

TOOTHED ARROW-WOOD. *Viburnum dentatum* L.

The common and latin names, of like significance, are appropriate for this shrub, the leaves of which are prominently toothed. It is said by the early botanist, Marshall, that the Indians preferred to use the young shoots of this species to those of any other of the arrow-woods for the fastening of their shafts. It is distinguished from the preceding form by its smooth branches and leaves, its larger size (five to ten feet), and its preference of moist soils. It is fairly frequent in swampy places. The flower clusters are two or three inches across, opening in early summer, and the blue-black berries, about one-fourth inch in diameter, mature in September. Although a native of wet places it will grow if planted in any good soil, and its pleasing habit and clean bright foliage combine with flowers and fruit to make it deserving of very general·use in ornamental planting.

WITHE-ROD. *Viburnum cassinoides* L.

This is a common shrub in swamps throughout the state. The name withe-rod is well chosen since its long lithe stems make the best of withes. It has an erect habit from five to twelve feet high, grayish bark and young branchlets, leaf stalks and under leaf surfaces sprinkled with rusty or scurfy dots. The leaves are thickish and dull green with apex somewhat tapering but dull-pointed and with margins varying from almost entire to dull-toothed. The leaf base tapers to the leaf-stalk and even

extends somewhat down it as a wing-like margin on either side.
The flowers open in early summer in rounded white clusters, two
or three inches across, and the berries, one-fourth inch long, ripen
in September to deep blue with bloom.   This is sometimes
planted as an ornamental shrub though it has no conspicuous
merit.   The fruit has a sweetish taste and may be eaten, though
few people gather it.

SHEEP-BERRY.   *Viburnum lentago* L.

This shrub, known also as nanny-berry or sweet viburnum,
is conspicuous in rich, moist woods, pasture thickets and along
streams.   Ordinarily of the size and habit of a shrub of five to

SHEEP-BERRY.
Fruiting branch, × ½.

ten feet, it may sometimes develop into a small tree of twelve to
eighteen feet.   The smaller stems and larger branches are of a

purplish-black color; the leaves are of a rich green tint and gracefully curved, rather large, margined with small sharp teeth and tapering to an acute point. The flowers open in June in large clusters, two to five inches broad. These, and the fruit cluster following, terminate the shoots and are sessile, i. e. have no extended common stem. The berries are the largest of this group, oval, one-half of an inch or more in length, and are borne in heavy clusters which often load the branches down with their autumn weight. They pass through a rich scarlet to a shining bluish-black with a bloom when ripe. The fruit is sweet and edible, and is better after being touched by frost. The foliage shows fine autumn tints. Altogether this is to be rated as one of the most attractive of our native shrubs for large decorative effects in landscape planting.

INDEX

Alder, hoary 24
Alder-leaved buckthorn 83
Alder, smooth 25
Alders, green 25
Alders, the 23
Alternate-leaved dogwood 95
Amelanchior 46
American hazelnut 27
American ivy 88
American yew 117
Ampelopsis 88
Appalachian cherry 43
Arbutus, trailing 114
Arrow-wood, downy 140
Arrow-wood Family 135-142
Arrow-wood, maple-leaved 139
Arrow-wood, toothed 140
Azalea 119
Azalea, pink 120
Balsam willow 20
Barberry, common 30
Barberry Family 30
Barberry willow 22
Beach heather 89
Beaked hazelnut 26
Beaked willow 20
Bearberry 101
Berries, the cultivated 60
Bilberries, the 104
Bittersweet, climbing 80
Blackberries 55
Blackberry 51
Blackberry, high-bush 58
Blackberry, mountain 58
Blackberry, recurved 58
Black blueberry 106

Black chokeberry 46
Black currant 37
Black crowberry 72
Black dewberry 60
Black raspberry 55
Black willow 16
Bladder-nut 82
Blueberries, mountain 110
Blueberry 51
Blueberry, Canada 106
Blueberry, common highbush..105
Blueberry, black 106
Blueberry, early low 107
Blueberry, late low 109
Blue honeysuckle 129
Bog bilberries 110
Bog willow 22
Bristly dewberry 59
Buckthorn, alder-leaved 83
Buckthorn Family 83-84
Buffalo-berry, Canadian 91
Bunchberry 94
Bush-honeysuckle 125
Button-bush 124
Canada blueberry 106
Canadian buffalo-berry 91
Ceanothus 83
Cherries 41
Cherry, Appalachian 43
Cherry, sand 42
Chokeberry 46
Chokeberry, black 46
Cinnamon rose 62
Cinquefoil 49
Climbing bittersweet 80
Climbing nightshade 122

Crowberry, black 72
Crowberry Family 72
Cultivated berries 60
Cultivated roses 66
Clematis, purple 28
Common barberry 30
Common elder 132
Common highbush blueberry..105
Common juniper 12
Cranberries, the 110
Cranberry-bush, high 137
Cranberry-bush, few-flowered..137
Cranberry, large 111
Cranberry, mountain 112
Cranberry, small 112
Crataegus 66
Creeping snowberry 103
Crimson rose, ... 66
Crowfoot Family 28-29
Cultivated berries 60
Currants 37
Currants and gooseberries......33
Damask rose 66
Daphne 91
Dewberries 55
Dewberry, black 60
Dewberry, bristly 59
Dewberry, red 59
Dewberry, swamp 60
Disk creeper 89
Dogwood, alternate-leaved 95
Dogwood Family 92-99
Dogwood, flowering 93
Dogwood, panicled 99
Dogwood, red-ozier 97
Dogwood, round-leaved 96
Dogwood, silky 97
Downy arrow-wood 140
Dwarf bilberry 110
Dwarf sumach 74
Early dwarf bilberry 74

Early low blueberry 107
Eglantine rose 66
Elder, common 132
Elder, red-berried 134
Elders, the 131
Fever bush 32
Few-flowered cranberry-bush..137
Flowering dogwood 93
Flowering raspberry 52
Fly honeysuckle 129
Forsythia 121
Fox grape 87
Fragrant sumach 76
French rose 66
Fringe tree 121
Gallic rose 66
Glaucous honeysuckle 128
Glaucus willow 20
Gooseberries 35
Gooseberries and currants....33
Gooseberry, prickly 36
Gooseberry, smooth 35
Gooseberry, swamp 37
Grapes, the 85
Great rhododendron 119
Green alders 25
Ground hemlock 13
Hairy honeysuckle 129
Hardhack 43
Hazelnut, American 27
Hazelnut, beaked 26
Hazelnuts, the 26
Heart-leaved willow 21
Heath berry 72
Heath Family 99-121
Heather, beach 89
Hemlock, ground 13
High-bush blackberry 58
High cranberry-bush 137
Hoary alder 24
Hoary willow 23

Hobble-bush 138
Holly family 78-80
Honeysuckle, blue 129
Honeysuckle, bush 125
Honeysuckle, hairy 129
Honeysuckle Family 125-135
Honeysuckle, fly 129
Honeysuckle, glaucous 128
Honeysuckle, swamp 129
Honeysuckle, tartarian 130
Huckleberry 103
India rose 66
Intricatae 69
Introduced shrubs, (privets,
  fringe-tree, forsythia, lilacs). 121
Introduction to new edition 2
Introduction 4
Ivy, poison 76
Japanese rose 66
Juniper, common 12
Juniper, red 13
Junipers, the 11
Kalmia 115
Key for determining identities. 6
Labrador tea 118
Late low blueberry 109
Large cranberry 111
Laurel Family 32-33
Laurel, mountain 117
Laurel, pale 118
Laurel, sheep 118
Laurel, the 115
Leather leaf 114
Leatherwood 90
Less common willows 22
Lilacs 121
Lonicera 127
Loosestrife Family 91-92
Loosestrife, swamp 91
Madder Family 123-125
Male berry 113

Maple-leaved arrow-wood......139
Maple Family 82
May flower 114
Meadow sweet 45
Mezereum Family 90-91
Moonseed 31
Moonseed Family 31
Mountain blackberry 58
Mountain blueberries 110
Mountain cranberry 112
Mountain currant 38
Mountain holly 79
Mountain laurel 117
Mountain shad-bush 149
New Jersey tea 184
Nightshade Family 122-123
Nightshade, climbing 122
Northern hoary willow 23
Oak Family 23-27
Oleaster Family 191
Olive Family 121
Pale laurel 118
Panicled dogwood 99
Pasture rose 64
Pine Family 11-14
Pink azalea 120
Poison ivy 76
Poison sumach 78
Potentilla 49
Prairie willow 20
Prickly ash 71
Prickly gooseberry 36
Privets 121
Psedera 88
Purple clematis 28
Purple osier willow 22
Pussy willow 20
Raspberries 51
Raspberry, black 55
Raspberry, flowering 52
Raspberry, red 52

Raspberry 51
Recurved blackberry 58
Red-berried elder 134
Red currant 37
Red dewberry 59
Red juniper 13
Red juniper, shrubby 13
Red-ozier dogwood 97
Red raspberry 52
Red-root, smaller 84
River grape 85
Rock-rose Family .... 89 -90
Rock shad-bush 47
Round-leaved dogwood 96
Rose Family .... 40 -70
Rhododendron 119
Rhododendron, great 119
Rhodora 121
Rhus 72
Rosa 61
Rosemary, wild 113
Roses, the 61
Rotundifoliae 69
Rubus 51
Rue Family .... 70 -72
Sambucus 131
Sand bar willow 23
Sand cherry 42
Saxifrage Family 33-38
Scotch rose 66
Service-berry 46
Shad-bush, mountain 49
Shad-bush, rock 47
Shad-bush, shore 47
Sheep-berry 141
Sheep laurel 118
Shining willow 21
Shore shad-bush 47
Shrubby cinquefoil 49
Silky dogwood 97
Silky willow 23

Slender willow 23
Small cranberry 112
Smaller red-root 84
Smooth alder 25
Smooth gooseberry 35
Smooth rose 65
Smooth sumach 74
Snowberry 126
Snowberry, creeping 103
Speckled alder 24
Spice-bush 32
Spirea 43
Staff vine 80
Staghorn sumach 73
Staff-tree Family 80-82
Steeple bush 44
Sumachs 72
Sumach, dwarf 74
Sumach Family 72-78
Sumach, fragrant 76
Sumach, poison 78
Sumach, smooth 74
Sumach, staghorn 73
Summer grape 87
Swamp dewberry 60
Swamp gooseberry 37
Swamp honeysuckle 129
Swamp loosestrife 91
Swamp rose 64
Sweetbrier rose 63
Sweet-gale Family 14-15
Sweet-fern 14
Sweet-gale 15
Table of contents i
Tartarian honeysuckle 130
Tea leaved willow 22
Tea, New Jersey 84
Tendril creeper 89
Tenuifoliae 69
Thornapples 66
Three-toothed cinquefoil 50

Toothed arrow-wood 140
Trailing arbutus 114
Twin-flower 125
Vine Family 85-89
Virgin's bower 28
Virginia creepers 88
Wayfaring tree, ... 138
Wild rosemary 113
Willow, beaked 20
Willow Family 16-22
Willow, heart-leaved 21

Willow, prairie 20
Willow, purple osier 22
Willow, pussy 20
Willow, shining 21
Willows, less common 22
Winterberry 79
Wintergreen 101
Witch-hazel 38
Witch-hazel Family 38-40
Withe-rod 140
Yew, American 13

NOTES

NOTES

NOTES

NOTES

NOTES